ON FOOT IN DUBLIN AND WICKLOW
Exploring the Wilderness

GW00599307

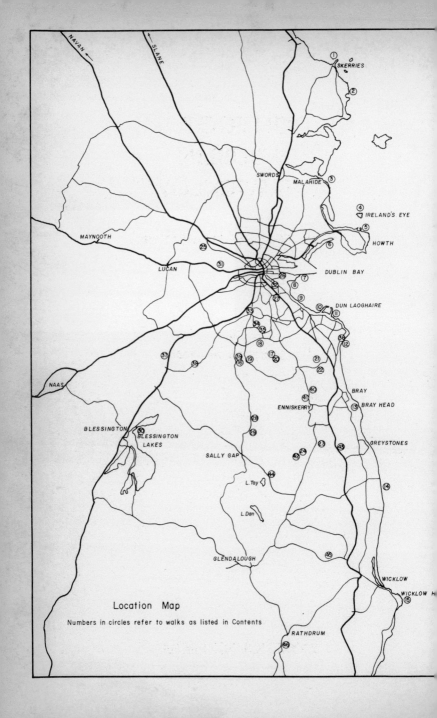

Location Map

Numbers in circles refer to walks as listed in Contents

ON FOOT
IN DUBLIN
AND WICKLOW

Exploring the Wilderness

by
Christopher Moriarty

WOLFHOUND PRESS

© 1989 Christopher Moriarty
Maps and illustrations © Wolfhound Press

First published 1989 by
WOLFHOUND PRESS,
68 Mountjoy Square,
Dublin 1.

British Library Cataloguing in Publication Data
Moriarty, Christopher
   On foot in Dublin and Wicklow : exploring
   the wilderness.
   1. Dublin (County). Recreations : Walking -
   Visitors' guides
   2. Wicklow (County). Recreations : Walking -
   Visitors' guides
   I. Title
   796.5'1'094183

   ISBN 0-86327-226-6

Cover design: Jan de Fouw
Illustrations: Jeanette Dunne
Typesetting: Redsetter Ltd., Dublin.
Printed and bound in Great Britain
by The Guernsey Press Co. Ltd., Guernsey, Channel Islands.

CONTENTS

PARKS AND FORESTS

Distances give the approximate length of each route,
either whole circuit or there-and-back.

INTRODUCTION

This is a collection of 46 routes: some short, some long, none arduous, for Dubliners and those who want to spend an afternoon getting away from it all. Most of them are as attractive to dogs and children as they are to discerning adults.

These are more than walks. Each route has something special to look at in the way of wildlife or landforms or castles and dolmens and things. Everybody knows that the scenery of Dublin and Wicklow is beautiful and that there are innumerable footpaths and hill walks. Indeed, there are many books to guide the wanderer.

This one is different in drawing attention to less obvious features and in offering explanations for aspects of the landscape so familiar to everyone that they are taken for granted. Within these pages you will find out why there are pink clouds in the pond in Herbert Park, why there are rocks on Three Rock, birds on Bull Island and fossils near Malahide.

The expanding city of Dublin has engulfed much of the countryside, but with surprisingly little damage to the wild places. Indeed, there have been real gains to the wanderer. State forests which were forbidding, fenced-in plantations have been transformed to welcoming parks. A number of private demesnes have been acquired by local authorities and opened to all. Riverside walks are being developed.

Each route has a map, advice on how to get there and whether it is good for dogs and children. The collection is based on articles which appeared in *The Irish Times* in 1982 and 1983, re-explored, revised and rewritten.

This book is an appetizer, with suggestions on where to begin to explore the rich wilderness that lies around Dublin. The routes combine a pleasant walk with information on plant or animal life, thoughts on the meaning of a bank of gravel or an outcrop of rock, memories of people who enriched the landscape, visions of the ice-covered landscape of ten thousand years ago. All leave their traces – recognizing these adds a dimension to the pleasure of a walk in the country.

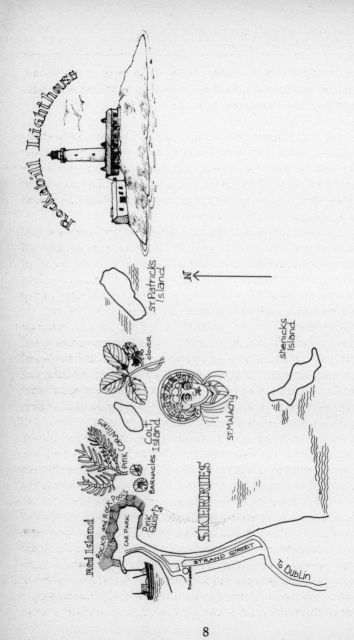

Rockabill Lighthouse

N ←

St. Patricks Island

Shenicks Island

clover

St. Malachy

Colt Island

Barnacles Island

Pink Coral

Aillins

Red Island

Rocks and Rock Pools

Car Park

Pink Quartz

SKERRIES

STRAND STREET

To Dublin

8

1   RED ISLAND

Skerries is clearly signposted off the Dublin to Belfast road, about 5 km north of Swords. It is a particularly safe seaside with no high cliffs. Best to visit at low tide.

Red Island is a promontory on the coast at Skerries, indeed the name of the town probably referred in the first place to the promontory. A skerry is a sharp sea rock and there are many rocks around Red Island, most of them sharp. The rock is of highly respectable antiquity, belonging to the Silurian era of some four hundred million years past.

You can begin a walk around the island from the monument at the northern end of the main street in Skerries where a side road leads down to the shore. Alternatively, you can follow a signpost for the harbour and drive past it to the car park. This road gives a wonderful view of the Mountains of Mourne and of the Cooley peninsula where Cuchulain defended the honour of Ulster.

The south side of the promontory marks the end of more than a mile of broad strand. The island to the south is Shenick's and you can walk out to it at low water over half a mile of almost level sand. A notice warns of the perils of being cut off by the tide. The rock of Shenick's Island is volcanic, contemporaneous with Lambay and millions of years older than the sandstones which compose Skerries and St Patrick's Island to the east.

Visitors are kept firmly to the foreshore by tall garden walls on the right. One of the gardens contains a remarkable summer house in the form of an ancient church. Nearby, just out of reach of the tide, a most uncommon wild flower grows. It is garden parsley, which must have escaped from one of the gardens and established itself as a self-perpetuating native.

The outcropping rocks dip gently towards the south, but have sharp pinnacles to the north, the skerries themselves. There are veins of quartz in the grey sandstone rocks: some of it pink coloured, possibly accounting for the name Red Island. Many of the rocks have been covered in concrete and surmounted by a maze of walls for the modest shelter of swimmers. A little bronze plate on the ground announces that this was the work of the "Skerries Visitors' Association 1902".

At the eastern tip of the island, the rocks are flat, almost like a pavement and stretch far out to sea. Sometimes seals come close in. There is a grey seal colony nearby on Lambay where breeding takes place in autumn.

The nearest of the islands is called Colt and it almost completely hides the larger one dedicated to St Patrick. A synod was held there in 1148, attended by 15 bishops, including St Malachy, and 500 priests. Their admirable purpose was that of 'establishing rules and morality for the laity'. Whatever its effects on the said laity, the synod led to a major revolution in the Irish church and its architecture.

A very interesting clover, *Trifolium occidentale*, grows at the tip of Red Island. It looks so similar to the common white clover that it was not identified as a separate species until 1961. The common clover has a sweet scent but the rare form has no scent at all. The first Irish specimens were found on Bray Head in 1979.

Round the corner, on the northern side of Red Island, the rocks at low tide show a series of bands of colour. Those nearest the shore are black, the next band is yellow and the lowest bright green. The black rocks are bare stone and stand just above the level of high spring tides.

The yellow ones are coloured by the myriads of barnacles which have cemented themselves to the rock surface. They thrive between the tides, where few other creatures, plant or animal, can compete with them in gaining a foothold. Strictly speaking the barnacles don't have a foothold. They lie on their backs and use their feet to catch their food.

The green of the lowest rocks is a plant growth. Amongst the green algae here there are lovely rock pools with gardens of seaweeds including the beautiful pink corralines. The final island for admiration is Rockabill, with its picture-book light-house built in 1860.

The road back to the town takes you past the harbour, a busy one with many fishing boats. They hunt the Dublin Bay prawns which live in burrows in the silt in deeper waters towards the north.

2 LOUGHSHINNY

Bus 33 to Rush passes within a mile of Loughshinny. Cars head for Rush, signposted on the Dublin-Belfast road. There is a signpost for Loughshinny in Rush. Bathing with lifeguard, cliffs safe for well disciplined children and dogs. Two km walk from car park to Martello Tower.

The cliff walk at Loughshinny leads around some of the most spectacular rock structures in Ireland to one of the greatest of the promontory forts. Even without these superlatives, the walk would make a very pleasant afternoon's relaxation. The 'lough' is a quiet and peaceful bay on the north Dublin coast, half way between Rush and Skerries and approached from either of them by a narrow road leading to a small fishing harbour.

The shelter given by the promontories has allowed rather silty sediments to accumulate so that the strand is, like that of Sandymount, firm and not altogether conducive to the building of sandcastles. With so many beaches nearby offering soft, cleaner sand, relatively few people go to Loughshinny and the coast is uncrowded even in good weather.

From the car park on the edge of the strand you can see a small outcrop of folded limestone to the left, while at the far side of the beach, stands one of the sections of cliff which has made the region geologically famous. The folded rocks form a colossal letter 'M', having been savagely compressed by the forces of the Hercynian mountain building two hundred and ninety million years ago. The rock was laid down in level layers in which pale grey bands of pure limestone alternate with black, shaley material. This makes the folding stand out vividly.

The Hercynian upheavals took place towards the end of the Carboniferous era and may be seen in Ireland on their grandest scale in the southwest, where they formed the parallel ranges of mountains and valleys of Kerry with their long sea inlets. Farther north, the Carboniferous strata are not so strongly folded and the crumpling of the cliffs of Loughshinny stands in sharp contrast to the less disturbed situation in the midlands nearby.

LOUGHSHINNY

CAR PARK

← TO RUSH

STRAND

PIER

Black Shales.

CLIFF PATH

EMBANKMENT
OF PROMENTORY
PORT

MARTELLO
TOWER

ROCK POOLS

CAVES

ROCK ARCHES

Around the car park and near the exposed rocks, a rather large plant with cabbage-like stalks and purple flowers grows. This is the tree mallow, an uncommon seashore species which has a special liking for the rocky parts of north County Dublin.

Walking along the strand brings you to the cliffs, first of all to rocks which are black and flakey, but still show the intense folding of the region. These, the Loughshinny black shales, are the youngest in the series and were deposited on top of the limestones which form the greater part of the cliffs. Above the shales there is a thick layer of gravel. It was carried there by the glacier which travelled down the Irish Sea from the north and spread over the low-lying coast.

The cliff path begins at the shale outcrop and takes a short cut between two stiles, leaving an earthen bank on the right and a field on the left. After crossing the second stile, you are properly in the world of the clifftop. Cattle are kept away from the edge by a continuation of the earth bank and the path runs through a mass of grasses, wild flowers and butterflies.

Turn left after passing a deep gully where there are traces of a building which apparently fell into the sea on a landslip. On the shore below, the core of one of the rock folds lies at the edge of the tide, smooth and shiny and looking like the back of a stranded swordfish. Stone steps beside a gate bring you into a cattle pasture where the great rampart of a promontory fort stretches for four hundred metres, cutting off fifteen hectares of clifftop from the mainland. Probably built round about the beginning of the Christian era, it remains an impressive earthwork two thousand years later on, still more than two metres high.

There is a lovely piece of rocky shore at the tip of the promontory, just beyond the Martello tower, reached by a slithery grass slope. The green of the dry land gives way suddenly to black rock and golden seaweed, draped in heaps amongst the rock pools.

At high tide the way back is by the cliff path, but at low water it is possible to scramble over the rocks at the cliff base and look at the caves where the inner parts of the rock arches have been eaten away. You might even tear your eyes away from the cliffs for a moment to look out to sea for seals and shelduck and many other seabirds.

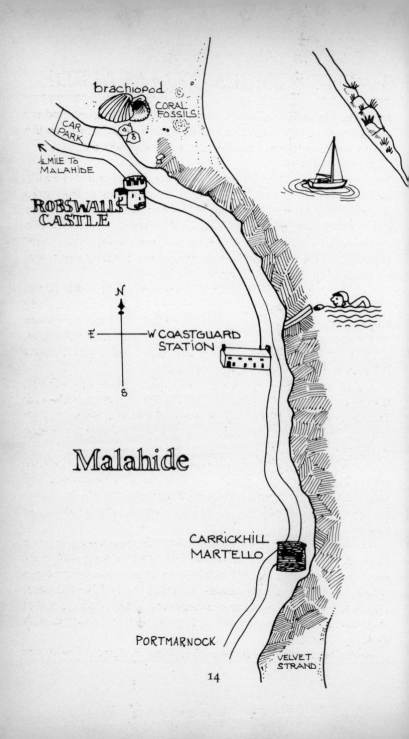

brachiopod

CORAL FOSSILS

CAR PARK

½ MILE TO MALAHIDE

ROBSWALLS CASTLE

N

E — W COASTGUARD STATION

S

Malahide

CARRICKHILL MARTELLO

PORTMARNOCK

VELVET STRAND

14

3 THE FOSSILS OF MALAHIDE

Bus 42 to Malahide and walk eastwards along the coast road for about 1 km. Lovely seaside for children and dogs; bathing in the channel slightly hazardous because of strong currents.

This is the best place in Dublin to look at fossils. For about a mile along the shore between Malahide and Portmarnock, grey rocks interrupt the strand. They form the most easterly outcrop of the Carboniferous strata which lie beneath most of the midlands and extend to the west coast. There are sandy beaches (and crowds) at both ends of the rocky part but, even on a fine Sunday afternoon, a feeling of space survives among the fossils.

A car park has been made by the foreshore, just south east of Malahide, set in the centre of a great green of immaculately mown grass. To the seaward side of it, the beach is so civilised that even the sand has been confined in cages. Within the bars, lyme grass grows on the sand and should in the course of time fix it firmly so that more lawn may be laid.

Across the channel are the sand dunes of Malahide 'Island', fine examples of how untamed nature wins land from the sea. The cages on the near side are essential because, even though sand dunes can survive wind and waves, they quickly get eroded by people.

Southwards from the car park you walk along the strand which, before long, is interrupted by the first ridge of limestone. The ridges become more and more frequent and eventually the scene changes from one of beach with rock outcrops to rock with small beaches.

A little to the north of Robswalls Castle, the beach is covered by the high tide which laps about the base of a retaining wall. Here the rocks have a number of brachiopod fossils, traces of creatures which bear a slight resemblance to cockle shells. Like the other fossils at Malahide, they are so firmly embedded in the rock that they can seldom be chipped out: you must be content with looking at them.

Immediately after the gents shelter, there is a high ridge of rock

15

followed by a low one. The low ridge abounds in fossil corals which look rather like cushions. Some show a pattern of small white circles, others are fan-like. These corals lived in colonies, each individual animal having a tube of its own, a little smaller than a cigarette. The pattern of white circles is made where the waves have eroded the fossil colony at right angles to the long axes of the tubes. The fans result where the tubes have been cut at a slant. On the same shelf of rock there is one much bigger coral, about 5 cm wide by 15 cm long with a ladder-like structure. This is *Caninia*, which you may find also on the banks of the Shannon and on the Sligo coast at Streedagh.

After the rock comes a small beach and then another bed of limestone, pale grey, much purer and therefore much more easily dissolved by the sea than the blackish stone. it has been worn into curious shapes with ridges and deep round hollows. As you continue southwards, the angle at which the rocks dip becomes more pronounced. The dip is to the north, giving a smooth, gentle ascent towards the south, ending abruptly in a sharp drop of a metre or so.

The dip angle steepens quite suddenly and, as soon as you pass the weed-covered rock, changes abruptly so that the downward slope now is towards the south. There is a geological fault at this point, where the strata were broken and forced out of alignment. But it is so difficult to see that the 19th century workers of the Geological Survey failed to record it.

The slope of the rock reverses once more to take a northerly dip below the next retaining wall. You then pass a bathing place where the concrete pier follows the line of a bed of black shale. Then there is a little bay with cliffs at the back, marking the position of the next fault. The strata leading up to it become more and more broken and then are suddenly replaced by completely different rock as you pass the fault line. This is the best place for brachiopods which abound in the pale brown broken stones on the shore.

Shortly afterwards, the scene changes as the Portmarnock Velvet Strand takes over from the rocky coast. Caravans, ice creams and people cluster near the domesticated martello tower and it is definitely time to return to more peaceful regions. You

can take a slightly different route back by following the footpath
that runs all the way above the rocky shore.

---

4   IRELAND'S EYE

**Bus 31 takes you to Howth Harbour. There you must search for
one of the motor boats which depart regularly in fine weather
from near the Yacht Club. Bird cliffs on the island are steep and
must be treated with great respect. Dogs should not be allowed
hunt the young birds.**

Landing on an island is always thrilling. The fact that the island
lies less than a mile from the shore and the ship is a motor vessel
crammed with people, dogs and picnic hampers, does nothing to
dull the sense of achievement as you clamber up the slithery,
weed-covered rocks to the soft turf and seagulls.

The boat lands at the north-eastern corner of the island, either
on the north or the east side according to the height of the tide.
A short climb brings you to a small piece of level ground near the
Martello Tower, crossing a patch of soft, peaty soil. Sea beet is the
dominant plant, its dark green, spinach-like leaves covering
much of the ground. Several other wild flower species, almost
unknown inshore, bloom in summer: sea pink with tufts of
slender stems with pink pom-poms, sea campion, with white
bells and the pink, star-shaped flowers of spurrey.

The rocks just to the west of the tower have breeding herring
gulls and the islet to the north, the Steer, is flat-topped and
packed with herring gulls and great black-backed gulls. June is
the best month to visit, when most of the eggs have hatched and
big, woolly chicks with lovely pepper-colouring wander in the
grass. Some young, non-breeding gulls are usually present,
distinguished by mottled brown colouring from the white and
silver adults. It takes four years for a herring gull to develop its
full colouring.

Walking westwards brings you over a bare patch of peaty soil, strewn with feathers. This is a roosting place for the gulls, where they gather to sleep and to preen. After crossing the bare patch, you pass a cleft in the rock, marking the line of a major geological fault. Then you come to the most approachable of the bird cliffs where kittiwakes, fulmars and razorbills nest. You may see puffins there, too, dumpy birds with clown-like white faces and multi-coloured bills. They disappeared from the island for thirty years, returning once more in 1986.

There are nests and eggs on almost every available ledge on the north side of the island, but at this point it is easy to get very close views of them. Although completely out of reach, the birds are only a few yards away and stay where they are as you watch them. In spite of their apparent tameness, it is kinder to move away from them before long.

A steepish climb brings you to the highest point of Ireland's Eye composed, like all the high points round about, of quartzite

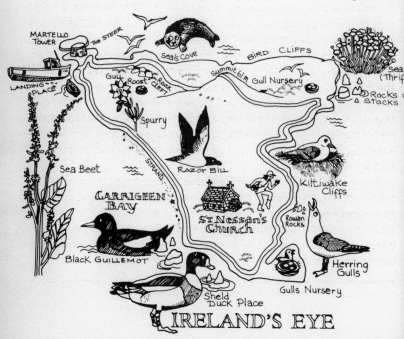

MARTELLO TOWER
THE STEER
SEALS COVE
BIRD CLIFFS
LANDING PLACE
GULL
Rock CLEFF
Roost
Summit 61m
Gull Nursery
Sea (Thrif
Rocks Stacks
Spurry
Sea Beet
STRAND
RAZOR BILL
CARRIGEEN BAY
St Nessan's Church
Rowan Rocks
Kittiwake Cliffs
Black Guillemot
Herring Gulls
Shield Duck Place
Gulls Nursery
IRELAND'S EYE

of Cambrian age. The view from the top is over the magnificent rock stacks to the east and down to the lowlands of the south of the island, where St Nessan's church stands amongst the bracken, the sole monument to a community which flourished on the island for 500 years or so from the 6th century.

Walking towards the stacks brings you through the main colony of herring gulls and great black-backs. The nests are large and easy to see, but you must tread carefully to avoid squashing the chicks which hide amongst the grasses or tuck themselves into rock crevices. To the south, the not so common lesser black-backed gulls nest. The stacks are densely crowded with nesting birds: all the species which nest on the other cliffs with guillemots in addition. When the young are fully grown, about the middle of July, the cliff birds move out to sea and few of them, except the big gulls, will be seen inshore until the following spring.

One of the most interesting ecological features of Ireland's Eye is the fact that there are no grazing animals. In their absence, a jungle of bracken and tall grasses grows up every summer. Interesting though it is, the jungle abounds in thistles and nettles and is uncomfortable to penetrate. It is therefore easier to walk all the way around the island than to beat your way across it. Many more of the cliff birds nest on the east side of the island including, sometimes, a pair of peregrine falcons. And on the west side, near the strand, there are usually shelduck, white duck with some black markings and orange sashes which nest in burrows in the sand dunes.

It is worth going to the island just for the strand, a wonderful stretch of clean sand, with lots of sea shells and a bank to shelter you from the east wind. Ireland's Eye makes a fair bid for first place among the treasures of the wilderness not just of Dublin but of Ireland: so much to see, so easy to get to and incredibly close to the centre of the fair city.

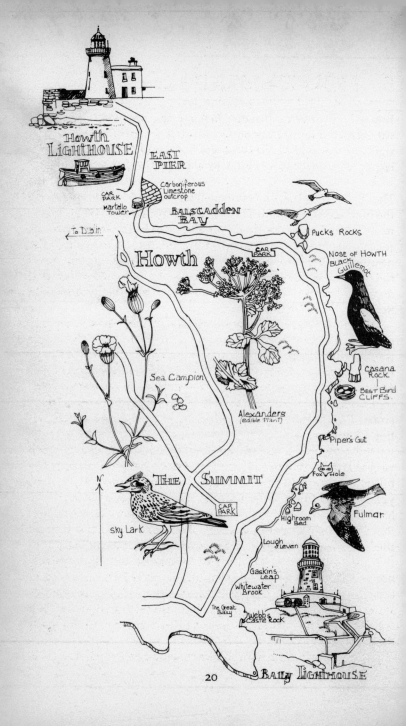

Howth
LIGHTHOUSE

EAST
PIER

Carboniferous
Limestone
outcrop

CAR
PARK

Martello
Tower

Balscadden
Bay

To Dublin

Howth

Pucks Rocks

CAR
PARK

Nose of HOWTH
Black
Guillemot

Sea Campion

Alexanders
(edible Plant)

Casana
Rock

Best Bird
CLIFFS

Piper's Gut

N

Fox Hole

THE SUMMIT

CAR
PARK

sky Lark

Highroom
Bed

Fulmar

Lough
Leven

Gaskin's
Leap

Whitewater
Brook

The Great
Baily

Webb's
Castle Rock

20

Baily LIGHTHOUSE

5   HOWTH HEAD

Bus No. 31 goes to Howth Harbour and you walk along the waterfront to reach Balscadden Road. The Cliff Path is a public right of way, very safe for dogs, but the cliffs themselves are highly dangerous. The path keeps a safe distance from them.

The cliff walk of Howth is the most remote and wonderful part of the mainland of Dublin. This is all the more remarkable, because in no place is it more than half a mile from the suburban bus route which encircles the Hill. Its magic lies in the fact that the narrow footpath runs between the sea on one hand and steep hills on the other. Hills and cliffs are too steep for motorbikes and domestic animals and therefore make a paradise of bracken, wild flowers and sea birds.

The route begins in Balscadden Bay which is just round the corner from the East Pier. The road rises steeply and from half way up the hill you can turn round and look northwards to the base of the pier where the sea breaks over the low-lying limestone rocks of Carboniferous age. To the south the character of the rock is completely different, with steep cliffs in place of level strata. Two hundred million years elapsed between the formation of the two.

The steep cliffs are the northern boundary in Ireland of the very ancient Cambrian rock which forms the main mass of the hill of Howth. The Cambrian era ended more than 500 million years ago. Between then and the Carboniferous, the Wicklow Mountains were built and the earth movements which raised them crumpled the Howth strata like a concertina. You can see the lines of the folding at several points along the cliff walk.

To the right of the road, the cliff is made of sand and pebbles, not of solid rock. This is glacial till, deposited by an ice sheet travelling down from the north. Most of the pebbles are of limestone, but there are a few purplish ones which may have been scooped up from Portrane where Old Red Sandstone strata reach the surface.

The dark green herb with shiny leaves and yellowish flowers is

21

Alexanders, established as a wild plant on the coasts of Dublin and Wicklow since the 18th century when it was a garden herb, used in salads. Alexanders fell from favour when celery was introduced.

Around the corner at the top of the hill, the road runs between wind-shaped sycamores on the left and cliffs of flaking shaly rock on the right. The first steep and tall hill rising above the upper car park is composed of quartzite, the extremely tough 'Howth Stone' which stands out above the softer shale and forms all the highest points of the peninsula. It is stained with iron oxides which provide the lovely golden colour.

The car park at the end of the road is dominated by a latter day round tower, built of Howth stone in the 1950s and serving for defence, not against any militaristic invader but from the more insidious noxious effluent of Dublin's populace.

There is always plenty to look at on the cliff walk, but the best time for a visit is between April and the middle of July when the wild flowers are in bloom and the cliff ledges are tenanted by thousands of seabirds. Early in summer, the fresh crop of bracken has not grown up and sheets of bluebells flower amongst the brown stems of the previous year's growth. The bluebells develop quickly in spring and complete their annual cycle before the bracken shades them out. Where the grass is short, the beautiful and rather rare little pale blue flower, squill, grows.

The cliff path leads eastwards from the car park, passing above the flat-topped islets called Puck's Rocks. The birds on them are mostly herring gulls, the commonest of the Dublin seagulls. Their wing tips are black with little white patches known as 'mirrors'. Herring gull chicks like to walk away from the nest within a few hours of hatching and therefore the parents prefer to nest on level spaces. Also present around Puck's Rocks, but much scarcer than the herring gull, is the great black-backed gull, a magnificent bird with a six foot wingspan.

On the cliffs to the east, fulmars and kittiwakes nest on small ledges; but they can be seen in much larger numbers and in great comfort at Casana Rock, half a mile farther on. The path from here goes quite steeply uphill and takes a sharp bend before flattening out at the 60-metre contour which it follows from the next mile.

The slope to the east is the Nose of Howth and the sea close by is discoloured by the aforementioned effluent. The sewer at this point runs in a tunnel below the Nose, an appropriate organ indeed for the purpose. The outfall is attended by a gathering of herring gulls, consuming unspeakable morsels.

For the next mile, the sole permanent artificial creations visible are the Kish lighthouse and occasional granite posts and concrete seats by the path. Bracken is the dominant plant, growing luxuriantly in spite of periodical bush fires. In early summer there are gardens of pink and white stonecrop and, in places, clusters of white burnet rose and purple bloody cranesbill.

The best bird cliffs are on the north-facing slope of the bay at Casana Rock. The massive, grey-green rock there is an igneous dyke, forced into the older rock in a molten state, perhaps at the same time as the volcanic eruption which formed Lambay. The steep, rocky cliff has many narrow ledges and nooks and these are just right to provide safe nesting places for the birds which spend the greater part of their lives far out at sea. The gulls are nearly all kittiwake, small and delicate and quite easy to distinguish from the herring gulls because their wingtips are black with no white mirrors.

Birds which resemble gulls, but have rather blotchy-coloured wings, enormous noses and big black eyes, are fulmar petrels. They are newcomers to Howth, having first nested there in 1955. They like to sail on the air currents, wings stiffly stretched out and scarcely moving. Finally there are two species of penguin-like birds: razorbills which are black and white, guillemots dark brown and white.

The next little bay gives a closer view of the kittiwakes, after which there is a relatively long walk where the slopes are too gentle to be safe for seabirds. The outward route ends at the wall of the lighthouse property on the Little Baily. From there you get a good view northwards along the cliffs of Howth and southwards to Wicklow Head and Bray Head with the great sweep of hills along Dublin Bay. There are many more bird cliffs around the Baily.

Other routes are available leading back to the car park. I often prefer to retrace my steps on the Cliff Path, if only for the lovely view over the harbour and Ireland's Eye which comes suddenly at the end. Alternatively you can go up the hill to the car park and take from there a footpath leading northwards across the moorland, rich with the song of skylarks. This path wanders gently back to the civilisation of the village of Howth, which begins where the lime-rich glacial till covers the ancient acid rock and allows gardens to be dug.

That was the wilderness part of Howth. But you mustn't forget the wonderful Howth Castle demesne a little way to the west of the harbour, inhabited by an ancient castle and an ancient family. Granuaile, it is said, paid a surprise visit there and was none too well received. The gardens contain a fantastic display of rhododendrons of many brilliant colours, cascading down the cliffs and one of the biggest dolmens in the country has stood there for four thousand years.

---

6   NORTH BULL ISLAND

Bus No. 30 has its terminus opposite St Anne's Park, about half a mile short of the causeway. In the interests of leaving the birds in peace, dogs should be exercised on the sand dunes, not in the salt marsh.

Howth is the oldest part of Dublin, its Cambrian strata laid down more than 500 million years ago. The head overshadows the youngest land, North Bull, which began to rise above the tide less than 300 years back and is still growing. The most amazing fact about them is that the sediments which hardened to form Howth so long ago were very much the same as those which now are building Bull Island.

The Bull developed initially from two or three small sand banks in the 18th century. Growth became rapid after the building of the North and South Walls of Dublin Port. The wooden bridge was built in 1819. By the 1950s traffic had increased to such an extent that the bridge became almost impassable on a fine Sunday so a causeway was built farther along the coast in 1965. This now provides the main access to the sand dunes and beach and our route begins beneath the beautiful signboard near the crossroads.

The Bull became Ireland's first bird sanctuary as long ago as 1931. In summer it is inhabited by thousands of birds but from late summer to midwinter, the numbers build up to tens of thousands as great flocks of wildfowl moved in from their breeding places far to the north of Ireland. From spring to autumn observant persons go to the Bull to see the wild flowers rather than the birds. And at any time anybody can get enormous pleasure from Dublin's most remarkable landform. In summer the joy of the safest strand in the country, in winter the pleasure of a walk by the sea where there is real space.

The Dublin Corporation has landscaped the ground close to the shore, laying out a green lawn sheltered by hedges of *Veronica*, one of few shrubs which can thrive in the salt-laden air. On the north side of the lawn the Santry River enters the lagoon through a culvert and flows seaward, broadening into Sutton Creek. Herring gulls always gather at the river close to the lawn for a swim. They like a supply of fresh, not salt, water to bathe in even though they are essentially sea gulls. The bed of the lagoon at this point is genuine Liffey silt, carried down into the Bay and swept by tidal currents around the tip of the Bull to settle where the flow is not so strong. Stretching out for half a mile from the causeway are sand flats, covered by glasswort plants, each a few inches high and looking rather like a candelabra.

There is a circle of lawn at the mid-point of the causeway and, when you pass this, you come to the beginnings of the salt marsh which runs the length of the lagoon. At this point, the marsh rises gently from the sand flats with no distinct margin. This shows that it is growing, slowly extending towards the deeper part of the lagoon. The most noticeable plant there is sea purslane, a very low shrub with pale, blue-green mealy leaves. It is especially interesting because it has invaded the marsh in less than thirty years. As recently as 1951 it was described as being very rare.

At high tide, the glasswort and many other interesting bits of Bull are covered by the water and, at high spring tide, the sea spreads over the salt marsh itself. Most of the birds rest at high tide some distance from the causeway. At low tide, the sand flats are fully exposed and the birds spread out over them to feed on the worms and shellfish and things that live in the sediments of the lagoon. My favourite time to arrive is about two hours before high water when the tide is driving the birds close inshore.

The route goes along by the edge of the salt marsh where there

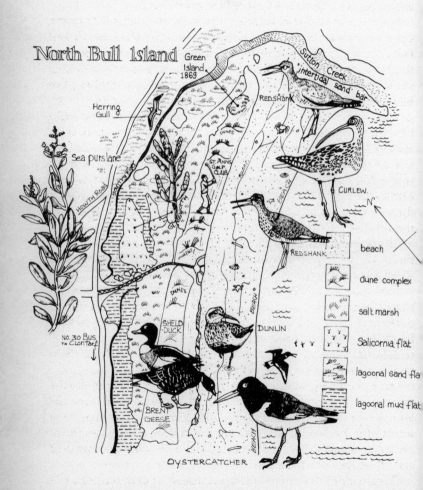

North Bull Island

Green Island 1869

Sutton Creek intertidal sand bar

REDSHANK

Herring Gull

Sea purslane

St. Anns Golf Club

CURLEW.

N

REDSHANK

beach

dune complex

salt marsh

Salicornia flat

SHELD-DUCK

DUNLIN

lagoonal sand flat

No. 30 Bus to Clontarf

lagoonal mud flat

BRENT GEESE

OYSTERCATCHER

26

are clumps of a special rice grass running in a line parallel to the shore. These were planted in or about 1934 in an attempt to reclaim the land. Fortunately, they belonged to a hybrid which was unable to spread and so they remain as a botanical curiosity.

Towards the north-east the outer edge of the salt marsh begins to lose its gentle slope and form a miniature cliff. This shows that the marsh is being eroded by the sea. So it is growing near the causeway and shrinking farther along the island.

Brent geese and shelduck are the most striking birds of the edge of the salt marsh. The brent geese have black necks and faces. They spend six months and more over the winter here and then fly off to remote Canadian islands to nest in the arctic summer. The shelduck give an impression of being white, but have black markings and chestnut collars. Many wading birds gather there for the winter: black and white oystercatcher and a bewildering collection of brown birds including redshank, curlew and knot. The latter is named in honour of good King Canute who, like them, defied the tide. The knot nest in Siberia so, with the brent geese, you have gathered in the same lagoon birds which travel to nest through 90 degrees of longitude in each direction – literally half way round the world, covering thousands of miles.

Although the island is not long, it is quite a vigorous walk to the tip by way of the salt marsh. Unless you keep to the inner side of the marsh, you will need to leap across or walk along the creeks which drain it. As you approach the tip you come to a circular sand dune, the oldest part of the island. At the tip, you can sit down and wait and watch while the birds come closer to you. But in summer there are notices begging you to keep away so as not to disturb the very beautiful and rare little terns which nest there on the ground.

The easiest way home lies along the old sand dunes where the grass is short and the ground is firm. After you have passed the windswept alders and willows you come, in summer, to a wonderful garden of wild flowers, including many species of orchid. Admire them, but don't pick them: some are rare and can't tolerate any such abuse.

The great problem with Bull Island is to curtail descriptions. It has already inspired three books and more than a hundred scientific articles. You might end your visit, or even begin it, by going to the Corporation's Information Centre a little way to the east of the Causeway.

It is open every day and staffed by very enthusiastic and helpful people. There is a beautiful video show, plenty of leaflets and a small library, to say nothing of an excellent display of posters.

---

7   THE SOUTH WALL

Bus No. 1 takes you to Poolbeg power station. Cars approach from the coast road through Ringsend. Wonderful dog-walk.

The great South Wall of Dublin port makes a delightful walk on a fine day. Perhaps because the approaches are hidden in deepest dockland, only a discerning few people wander along the wall so that it is a peaceful haunt of birds and passing ships.

But it is strictly for fine weather. The Port and Docks Board tell you this in a notice which states that 'persons who walk along the wall' are in danger of being swept off 'in adverse tidal or bad weather conditions'.

The approach to the Wall from Sandymount or Irishtown takes you past the cheerfully coloured houses to the Ringsend power station and oil storage tanks. A good road passes along the formidable security fence which surrounds Poolbeg power station with its slender chimneys and has encaged the former Pigeon House hotel. You can drive on to the pier itself but, if you stop at the car park on the east side of the security fence, you have the added attraction of a small patch of sandy beach.

This has been formed where the outer border of the car park meets an older portion of shore. In the angle between the two, fine, clean sand has blown in to form a small silvery beach with sea shells, a sort of oasis in a desert of tidal flats. Just above the reach of the tide, blue-green lyme grass grows in the sand. Its roots tie up the sand grains, protecting them from the wind. Ultimately, soil will form and clovers and different grasses will oust the lyme.

Most of the seashells are cockles, the last mortal remains of molluscs which enjoyed indolent lives buried just below the surface of the sand flats between the tides. The shore is protected by a line of enormous quarried boulders, most of them granite, but a few of dark greenish volcanic rock, probably andesite from the northwestern Dublin mountains which you can see in the distance.

At the edge of the beach there is often a thick mat of the alga *Enteromorpha*. When it is alive, this weed forms a green coating over the sand flats in the shallow parts of Dublin Bay. Brent geese from Bull Island come to feed on it in spring. In summer, wind and waves gather it up and deposit it to form a crusty carpet in certain places. Eventually it gets broken up and scattered again to form food for the lugworms which will in turn be recycled by curlews and bass and bait-catchers.

The walk along the breakwater begins at the stone-built house with barred windows which contains the pumping machinery for propelling treated sewage into the river when the tide is falling. Many black-headed gulls rejoice in this provision of abundant, if unmentionable, food. Within the harbour at this point a platform with a lighthouse stands in mid-channel. The platform has been appropriated as a nesting place by a colony of terns.

The first embankment on the line of the breakwater was begun in 1711 and made from wooden piles and gravel. After fifty years or so, it had been breached in several places and the building of the present stone structure began. The building took nearly 30 years and was completed in 1796. The sides and paving are made from rectangular blocks of granite measuring about 30 cm by 120 cm. They enclose a core of rough granite blocks and gravel.

On the south side of the wall a border of stones and rusting iron bars extends about 20 metres out from the wall. These are the first of a series of outer protections which reduce the force of the waves at the base of the wall. Four hundred metres farther on, the iron bars cease and boulders alone are used. For the next 200

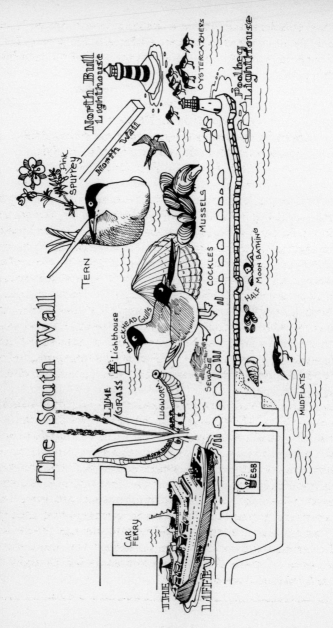

The South Wall

North Bull Lighthouse
North Wall
Pink Spurrey
Oystercatchers
Poolbeg Lighthouse
Tern
Mussels
Cockles
Half Moon Bathing
Lighthouse
Blackhead Gulls
Sewage
Lime Grass
Lugworm
Mudflats
Car Ferry
E58
The Liffey

30

metres boulders and wall are festooned with mussels, after which dense seaweed takes over. A tribute to the power of wind and wave is provided by a notice on the wall of the Half Moon bathing place:

DANGER
Swimmers Beware
Rocks under water due to Hurricane Kay 1988.
Persons who swim here do so at own risk.
Half Moon SC. Founded 1898

The bathing place occupies the site of a former shore battery and provides the only shelter on the wall. Farther on, the smallish rocks on the outer side of the pier are replaced by bigger boulders as the wall gradually becomes more exposed to the force of the sea. The Poolbeg lighthouse itself is bordered on its seaward side by enormous lumps of iron-bound masonry which have been torn away and pushed around in the course of two centuries.

From the end of the pier there is a pleasant view of Howth to the north and the Dublin mountains to the south. You can see the TV mast on Kippure and from that you can, at least in theory, gaze down on the source of the Liffey. So the beginning and end are visible from the one spot: a rare happening for a river 80 miles long.

In summer terns fish at the edge of the tide and oystercatchers hunt for cockles on the sand flats. Later in the year the terns move south, but many more oystercatchers and thousands of other wading birds of many species come to feed on the worms and shellfish which burrow in the sand between the tides. Sometimes seals appear close to the pier and in winter mergansers, great-crested grebes and red-throated divers hunt for small fishes. There are even wild flowers to be found on the granite paving, especially the little pink-flowered spurrey which grows amongst the crevices.

The return journey is simple, as indeed was the outward. Diversions of more than fifteen metres to left or right end abruptly in mud, rock or water.

8 SANDYMOUNT STRAND

Car park is on Strand Road, north of Sandymount Tower. Bus No. 3 from town. For complete safety the trip should be made when the tide is falling. Ideal for dogs and children.

The devotees of Sandymount Strand engage in exercising dogs or ponies and in digging lugworms. Although the sea is too shallow for bathing, it confers on native and visitor alike the incomparable benefit of preserving from developers an immense open space.

A flight of steps at the northern end of the car park leads down to the strand, passing through a gap in the break-water of massive blocks of dark volcanic rock. A little way out from the steps there stands a notice erected by the Corporation of Dublin to warn its citizens of the perils of proceeding beyond a distance of 250 yards. When the tide is rising there is a very real risk of being cut off and facing an unpleasantly wet return to the land.

Heaps of shells lie along the shoreline at the breakwater. They are the last mortal remains of burrowing molluscs which live below the surface of the sand. Most of them are cockles, with a good few razor shells and occasional tellins, their delicate shells marked by hands of rose pink colour.

From the steps you walk in a straight line towards the tall chimneys of Poolbeg generating station. The sand is fine and firm and arranged in ridges which run parallel to the shore. The ridges are high enough to enable you to walk dryshod across the damp patches. Lugworm casts, small conical mounds of grey sand, are plentiful; about twice as many in the wet places as there are in the dry ones.

The straight passage to the chimneys is broken by a runnel which begins at a freshwater stream close to Sandymount Tower. You can follow the runnel to the edge of the tide, passing on the way two mounds of shelly gravel which stand up above the surrounding sand flats. Between them lies an area where sand mason worms live. They construct little tubes of sand grains which stand an inch or two above the ground. When the tide comes in, the worms poke their heads out through the tubes and snap up microscopic creatures from the water.

The runnel turns right handed to go towards the sea, parallel to the embankment near the power station. Birds become more plentiful as you approach the edge of the tide. In summer, black-headed gulls and terns are the most abundant. In winter, the gulls remain and are joined by thousands of wading birds of many species: redshank, dunlin and oystercatcher are always there and sometimes, particularly in early spring, brent geese come across from their favourite haunt on the North Bull.

As it approaches low tide mark, the runnel begins to zig-zag with increasing vigour, struggling to retain its identity as long as possible before surrendering to the anonymity of the open sea. When you meet the tide you turn left to go towards the embank-

ment, a former tip heap protected from the waves by enormous chunks of masonry. Access to the embankment is barred by a deep gut which runs nearly all the way to its shoreward end.

Just where the gut dries out, tidal currents have created a miniature mountain landscape of smooth hillocks, a few inches in height, replacing the long lines of parallel ridges. These little hills make an oval fringe surrounding a level space. Evidently an exceptionally good feeding ground for the birds, it is pock-marked by innumerable beak stabs.

At this point you can leave the sand and walk along the embankment at the edge of the reclaimed land. The border between this and the wilderness of sand flat is abrupt, but nature survives in one little corner between the embankment and Beach Road. There a sand dune is trying valiantly to establish itself, with a band of seashells, some fine white sand and a few clumps of lyme grass. Time alone will tell whether the local authorities or marine currents will win the race to fill in this part of Dublin Bay.

---

9   BOOTERSTOWN SLOB

Buses 5, 6, 7 and 8, among others, serve Booterstown. Dogs should not be encouraged to rampage amongst the ducks, but the strand at low tide is great for them and for ponies and children.

The rushy swamp, tucked in between railway line and main road, looks like the last remnant of a natural habitat on the southern side of Dublin Bay. In fact, although now a highly respectable and valued wilderness, it is an entirely artificial creation. The term 'slob' generally refers to reclaimed land of this kind.

The Dublin and Kingstown railway line, completed in 1834, ran across the strand from Merrion Gates to Blackrock. The embankment built to carry it prevented the normal flow of tides and, in the course of time, a marsh developed on the landward side. It was described by Weston St John Joyce in 1912 as a 'foul-smelling salt marsh'. That was before our enlightened days of ecological tolerance and now the Slob, conceivably much improved odoriferously since Joyce's time, is a treasured wildlife sanctuary, held under lease by An Taisce.

The route, which is a very short one, begins at the corner of the car park south of the railway station. A group of slightly under-nourished sycamore trees stands by the edge of the car park. They seem to be 20 or 30 years old and the gorse bushes nearby are probably about the same age. It is likely that the ground was too wet for gorse and sycamore before that.

Buddleia trees have joined the shrubbery more recently. A

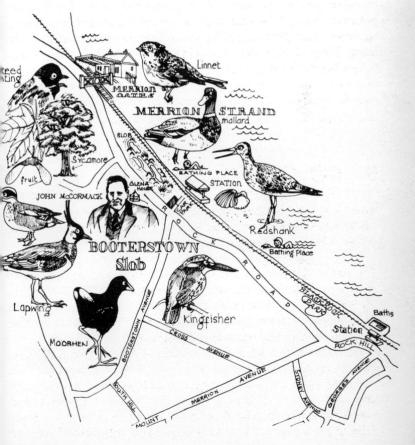

35

beautiful poster, the work of Nora McGuinness, depicting a lapwing and some duck, announces that the area is a bird sanctuary.

You can walk beside the road, along the top of the embankment to the viewing point which stands opposite to a large house with a pointed, gothic roof. This house, Glena, was built a short time after the advent of the railway when old farmhouses were replaced by suburban dwellings for affluent citizens. John McCormack lived there and is commemorated by a stone plaque on the wall.

At the viewing point there is a picture, by Gerrit van Gelderen, of the principal birds of the area. Mallard and moorhen stay on the pond throughout the year and in winter teal come in. These beautiful little duck can seldom be as easily approached as at Booterstown and you can admire the emerald green cap decoration and yellow pants of the drake. At high tide in winter, redshank, lapwing and oystercatcher gather to roost at the water's edge.

The tall rushes, brown and dead but still upstanding in winter, are the sea club rush *Scirpus maritimus*. They have been known to grow by the seaside at Sandymount and Merrion since 1794 when Dr Walter Wade identified them and listed them in his book on the native plants of County Dublin. If you scramble down the steep embankment and splash across the damp grass to look closely at the pond you will be greeted by wisps of snipe, rising noisily from the marsh. Neither teal nor snipe nor sea club rush are rare things in Ireland, but they are almost unknown in the south Dublin suburbs and therein lies the great importance of Booterstown.

Following the footpath towards the northwest brings you past two interesting articles of street furniture. The first is a roughly carved pillar of granite, saying that it stands 4 miles from Dublin and 3 miles from Kingstown. The second is a seat with the following inscription.:

Booterstown Ladies Club
To mark their 25th year
1962-1987

The boundary of the slobland is a concrete culvert which provides a footpath towards the seashore. Reed buntings can often be seen from the culvert and the wasteland to the north has plenty of annual weeds which go to seed and provide food for linnets. The culvert carries storm water to a tidal channel where kingfishers perch. In the days before DART it used to be possible to cross the railway line and reach the strand. Nowadays you must content yourself by gazing at the sand flats from the concrete roof of the drain. If you want to gain the strand you must go back and cross the railway by the footbridge.

The sand is firm and fine, except for a soft and sinking bit where the culvert discharges. Shells of razor fish and cockles abound, but there are few mussels or other seashells. Just after the tide begins to fall, the redshanks and oystercatchers leave the sloblands and go to hunt on the sand, close to the sea wall. Then they follow the receding tide to the distant outer edge of the sand flats, more than half a mile away.

At the culvert, the sea wall is made mainly from granite blocks, hewn from Dalkey Quarry and transported by rail. Curiously, no seaweed is attached to them at this point, though it appears as you go southwards towards the railway station. Closer to the station and the forlorn bathing place, the granite blocks are replaced by limestone: the black rocks which give their name to the nearby township. A few of these blocks display white fossils: circular crinoid stems and cockle-like brachiopods. They lived at the bottom of a clear, tropical sea nearly three hundred million years ago in the Carboniferous era.

---

10   WEST PIER, DUN LAOGHAIRE

Buses 7 and 8 stop near Top Hat ballroom. Car parking on roadside or on the pier, approached by bridge to the east.

The West Pier is a noted habitat of ornithologists, fisherfolk and free-range dogs. The more genteel East Pier has fewer birds for the watching and an ordinance requiring the leashing of dogs. The West Pier is 1,500 metres long, measured from its base at the railway crossing.

From the Coal Quay bridge, the land slopes downhill towards the west and levels out after 50 metres. There is a factory across the road from the harbour, overlooked by houses at a much higher level. The factory occupies the head of the creek which formed the old natural harbour of Dunleary. Behind a pair of rusty iron chimneys, a grass-covered cliff marks the former coastline. There was a breakwater in the 18th century, but that harbour silted up and the safety of the anchorage was impaired. The great days of Dunleary began in 1817 when the first stone of the modern harbour was laid. The West Pier was begun in 1820 and completed in the 1840s.

The base of the wall of the Coal Harbour is festooned with seaweeds. At low tide they hang limply, but when the water rises

WEST PIER, DUN LAOGHAIRE

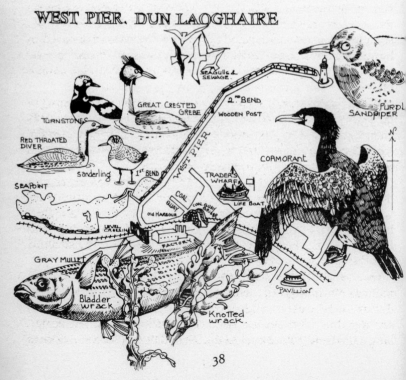

38

they spread out near the surface, supported by air bladders. The golden-brown kind is bladder wrack. A second species is the knotted wrack with blackish and much bigger floats. A hair-like red seaweed with no floats of its own lives attached to the knotted wrack. When the water warms up in spring, grey mullet return to the Coal Harbour from deeper parts and cruise lazily backwards and forwards along the wall or, sometimes, leap playfully into the air.

After passing the Dun Laoghaire Motor Yacht Club on the main pier, there is a little gateway on the left leading down the steps to a smaller breakwater. The wall at this point is relatively high and bears a forbidding coping containing broken glass. It is by no means clear what particular race of vandals this was supposed to deter – or why they would ever have wanted to cross the barrier.

Just beside the gateway, a singularly gnarled elder bush has somehow survived the salt spray for 30 or 40 years. Farther out on the pier, anywhere that the smooth stonework has been broken, some bush or other manages to grow. Small land birds such as linnets often come to the bushes and butterflies abound in fine weather: painted ladies, red admirals and peacocks among others.

When the tide is out, a patch of fine sand appears, stretching as far as the First Bend of the pier. A small flock of wading birds comes to feed there in winter. It includes redshank, dunlin, sanderling, curlew and oystercatcher and this is one of the best places in Dublin Bay for a close look at them.

Just beyond the First Bend, a flight of steps leads down to a little rocky promontory. This is a favourite spot for turnstones which arrive to feed there as soon as the tide begins to fall. They have beautiful mottled chestnut plumage and orange legs and live by turning over fronds of seaweed to hunt for the shrimps and things that hide beneath them.

Out to sea to the west, the water is shallow, less than six metres. All through the winter it is inhabited by a collection of diving birds: great crested grebe, red-throated diver and cormorant together with several species of duck: merganser, scoter, long-tailed and goldeneye. At the Second Bend you come close to a sewage outfall where various things are released when the tide falls. Gulls like them and a great flock gathers daily for this unsavoury feast. Occasionally an Iceland gull joins the gathering and stays around for weeks.

The 9-metre sounding runs northwards from near a point marked by a wooden post. To the east of it, in the deeper water, diving birds are scarce in winter, but in summer razorbills, guillemots and black guillemots appear from time to time. At any time of the year, seals and porpoises may turn up.

Along the final, straight portion of the pier you can walk on the outer side. Occasionally gannets fly past, but the special bird of the West Pier is the purple sandpiper. This is a species of very strictly defined feeding habits and finds nearly all of its food amongst the seaweeds at the very edge of the tide. Its specialisation makes it a rare bird on the Irish coast, with the West Pier one of its few favoured haunts.

Buildings replace birds as objects to marvel at when you reach

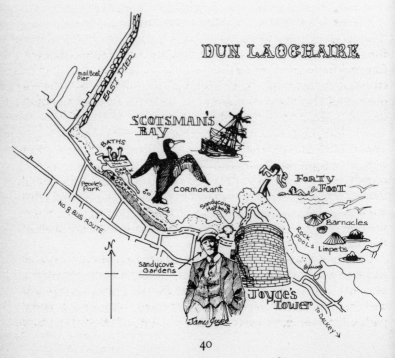

the end of the pier. The lighthouse was built in the mid-1850s and followed by a keeper's house in 1863. Both are made of granite, cut with almost unbelievable skill and beautifully finished with carved mouldings. The paving around the light-house has a delightful fan-pattern.

Such is the West Pier of 1989, little changed for generations. If you want to know more about its ancient state, read Peter Pearson's delightful book 'Dun Laoghaire Kingstown'. And for the future, follow the daily papers. Much will change and marinas may push the birds a little way farther into Dublin Bay but, hopefully, citizens and dogs will continue to be free to promenade upon the breakwater as they have done for more than a century and a half.

11   SCOTSMAN'S BAY TO SANDYCOVE

Bus No. 8 travels along the main road parallel to the coast road. Car parking is best beside the Baths, other places tending to be crowded in fine weather. A delightful seaside for a sedate walk or zoological exploration – not too good for sandcastles or vigor-ous exercising of free-range dogs.

The coast to the east of Dun Laoghaire Harbour is a mixture of ruggedness and respectability. It once was a rocky shore, but the rocks have been covered in with paving, car parks and lawns so they emerge only in isolated places. It is difficult to picture this as a terrifying coast on which unknown numbers of sailing ships were wrecked before the present harbour was built for them in the 1820s.

The route begins at the base of the East Pier where footpaths and a rock garden of limestone blocks were laid out early in the present century. Down at sea level the granite bedrock is exposed and there is a small area of shingle beach, composed of equal parts of granite and limestone pebbles. The path along the shore is interrupted by the bathing place, opened in 1843 as the Royal Victoria Baths and rebuilt between 1905 and 1911.

Following the wall on the east side of the baths brings you back to the sea front and a view from above of deep rock pools. The pools here, however, are slightly inaccessible and there are more and better ones at the Fortyfoot.

The way now goes along a footpath, just above the rocks. Bird life in Scotsman's Bay is limited, compared with the variety which can be seen from the West Pier. The reason is that the water is considerably deeper. The 3 fathom line comes close inshore and the various ducks and other birds which hunt for their food on the seabed find it beyond comfortable reach. Likewise, wading birds are scarce because there is very little tidal mud or fine sand.

The most regular visitors are the cormorants which regularly alight on the rocks and hang their wings out to dry. The majority of swimming and diving birds can stay at sea indefinitely, but the feathers of cormorants get wet too easily and they have to come out on dry land several times a day.

Now that the sailing boats can take shelter in the harbour, the sea vents its rage on the breakwaters and footpaths which have attempted to displace it. The path is broken in many places and chunks of masonry on the foreshore tell of past victories of the waves. A little farther on, the footpath ends abruptly in a wall and the walk is continued either by scrambling over the rocks at low tide or, more comfortably, by climbing up steps which bring you to the road and on to the pleasant gardens at the disused and delapidated Sandycove Baths.

The garden rambles over soil derived from glacial gravel which elsewhere along the sea front is hidden by the road and the houses. From the garden, maintained in impeccable order by the local residents, you may go downhill to the neat little harbour of Sandycove, passing an exposed piece of the glacial gravel just beyond the high wall.

The road crosses the base of a promontory below James Joyce's Tower and from there you may go down to the rocks beside the Fortyfoot, a perfect foreshore for hunting for small sea beasts. The granite slopes gently down to the lowest tide level. Rock pools abound and you can trace a gradual succession of living things down to the shore line. Barnacles and limpet live at the highest levels, along with tiny species of periwinkles. All are able to seal their openings when the tide falls and so maintain a marine environment within their shells. They are remarkably tough creatures, able to endure wet and dry, hot and cold, to say nothing of the buffeting of the waves. It may not look that way on a summer's day, but the rocky shore is one of the harshest habitats in nature.

---

12   WHITE ROCK

The route starts just north of Killiney railway station. The nearest bus is the 45A from Dun Laoghaire to Ballybrack, whence you walk down the Military Road and turn left for the public car park below the hotel. The beach is almost inaccessible to cars and ideal for free-range dogs and children.

White Rock, which marks the northern end of Killiney beach, is part of a scene of ancient turmoil. The steep, wooded slopes of Killiney Hill, plunging down to the rocky cliffs mark the region where Caledonian granite 400 million years ago forced its way as molten rock into the older Orovician strata. The lower, grass-covered cliffs to the south are of glacial till: stones, sand and clay deposited when the Irish Sea basin was a southward-flowing sea of ice.

You leave the car park through a dank subway which opens suddenly to the strand and pounding surf. The sea there is making a determined effort to remove the coast. The railway, built in 1854 on the cliff of glacial debris, stands about fifteen metres above the tide, safe from the waves but threatened by erosion of the cliff beneath. To protect the cliff, a bastion of stones secured in cages of wire mesh, was built and a lawn and footpath have been laid out behind it.

The sea has removed the clay from the glacial till and left the

43

beach strewn with a rich variety of pebbles, smooth and rounded. Most of them are dark grey limestone which has been carried at least seven miles from the north and probably a great deal more. There are granite pebbles of several shades of grey from Killiney or Dalkey and an occasional piece of pink granite from the Mountains of Mourne. Reddish sandstone and conglomerate come from near Portrane. A bluish stone with white flecks is Lambay porphyry and a yellowish one is Antrim flint. Experts can find bluish microgranite all the way from Ailsa Craig.

The route goes northwards along the bastion which ends at a point where the beach is being built up, not eroded. The coarse lyme grass which grows there anchors the sand and may eventually help to establish firm soil. This grass is quite a new arrival, not there in 1904 when Nathaniel Colgan published his 'Flora of County Dublin'. Lyme grass at Killiney was recorded for the first time by J. P. Brunker in 1939.

Cliff and railway line gradually rise to about 30 metres above the sea as you approach the hamlet of beach huts entitled 'TEAS'. In winter the tea-room houses more lobster pots than people, but you can hire boats there in summer. Below the tea-room you meet the first of the large granite boulders, dumped there by a local glacier which flowed over Killiney Hill.

Then the first outcrop of rock looms and you must take a fairly easy climb unless you prefer to slither over the weed-covered rocks below. To the north the outcrop is yellowish granite but it joins a band of grey-green schist, formed where the molten granite baked the older sedimentary rock. At White Rock the junction between granite and schist appears again. Apparently, tongues of granite pushed their way into the older strata. The steep slopes here mark the very edge of the Wicklow granite mass.

A deep cleft in the hillside forced the railway men to build a splendid viaduct with granite facing and red brick arches. Drainage holes between granite blocks are occupied by fulmar petrels which first came to Killiney in the 1950s. They spend the winter at sea, gliding over the waves and never coming to land. But springtime in a fulmar's life is an early happening and they move in to the nest sites before the end of January.

The schist at the base of the viaduct has a starry pattern, the points of the stars being crystals of andalusite. The slopes of the earth-covered cliffs at White Rock are covered with a naturalised garden flower, *Senecio cinerea*. Its ancestors came in a packet of seeds planted at Sorrento Cottage in 1875. They grow in profusion in this bay, their silver-green leaves contrasting with the greens and browns of native plants. The truly remarkable thing about them is not that they are there, but that they have not succeeded in spreading any further. They must be confined to White Rock by some subtle influence of micro-climate.

The return journey along the beach is lovely for its distant scenery of Bray Head and the Sugarloaves. Alternatively you can climb 287 steps to the Vico Road above.

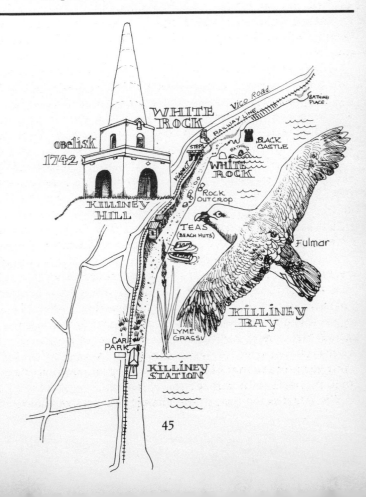

13   BRAY HEAD

Bus 45 or DART to Bray, followed by a walk along the Esplanade. Cars can park near the amusement arcade, but parking is fairly congested on a fine Sunday. Cliff walk is safe for well-disciplined dogs and children: safety walls can be climbed easily and the cliffs are very steep in places. Cliff path gives a gentle walk, higher slopes are more exacting. About four miles round trip.

The Bray Head cliff path takes you with satisfactory speed from seaside squalor to two miles of wilderness. It is a slightly tamed sort of wilderness, furnished with a footpath and a safety wall and carved up in places by heroic railway engineers. But cliffs remain to this day the only part of Ireland untransformed by agriculture or industry.

The starting place is the car park at the southern end of the Esplanade. The shingle beach on the left is made up mainly of limestone pebbles, with purple sandstones and some granite: all of it washed out from the glacial till at the base of the cliffs. The ice moved down the Irish Sea basin, spreading out over the lowlands and skirting Bray Head. Just up the hill to the right, the till is being eroded so quickly that old field drainage pipes are revealed.

Round the corner, the concrete path forks, the left hand going to a delapidated bathing place, the right crossing the railway bridge. There is a deep cleft in the rock on the right which has provided enough soil and shelter for a slightly marshy wood to develop, with elder, oak and sycamore.

Beyond them there is a plantation of pine and spruce on the upper slopes and on the cliff path itself a fine exposure of the colourful rocks which form most of the Head. They are green and purple slates, with added colour in the form of little patches of a brilliant yellow-green lichen, looking like splodges of paint.

The rocks of the Bray Series are the oldest in Dublin and Wicklow, belonging to the Cambrian era which ended more than 530 million years ago. Muddy sediments accumulated on the floor of a sea basin which extended from Wexford to Wales. In the course of time the sediments solidified and were subjected to such intense pressure that the rock developed its slatey form.

On the rocks below the path, herring gulls begin to occupy their nesting sites in March and, close by, fulmars fly to and fro. Just beyond the first shelter the rock is quite different: instead of being slatey it is massive and coloured pale pinkish brown, with veins of white quartz. This is quartzite, formed from fine sand rather than from mud. It is so much harder than the slate that it stands out to make all the high points and major promontories of Bray Head.

From the ruined house nearby, you can look back towards Killiney, over the bright green golf links of Woodbrook, laid out on the easily-drained and rich soil formed on the glacial till. Then you go onwards to the south side of the Head and the view is

towards Greystones and Wicklow Head.

Many birds live on the cliffs towards the south. Kittiwakes make themselves heard with trisyllabic squawks, in contrast to the wailing of the herring gull and stentorian snore of the fulmar. Ravens circle up above and razorbills sit in the water below. Looking back, there are two railway tunnels: the outer one abandoned along with a series of cuttings found to have been placed just a little too daringly close to the edge of the cliff.

After passing a second quartzite cliff, you come in sight of Cable Rock where an abandoned wartime observation post is slowly decaying. Up the hill from it, a tripod marks a convenient place to cross the wall. Quartzite cliffs tower above on the skyline, looking deceptively like the summit of the Head. Below them live some splendidly wild goats. The ascent of the cliff is rather gorsey and brambly, but the going is easier once you have gained the higher ground. The real summit is about a quarter of a mile from the cliff-top and from there you can take a gentle walk over the moorland to the Holy Year cross. The outcrops of quartzite are high and covered with heather, while the slates underlie lower ground with a mantle of bracken and moorland grasses.

A steep descent from the cross goes through a pine wood and down to the joys of busy Bray.

---

14   THE BREACHES

Bus 84 to Kilcoole goes a short way down the road (turning off at Byrne's Bar and Lounge) from Kilcoole to the beach; cars can park at the seaside. A delightful walk for children and dogs, but watch out for occasional trains which cannot be heard above the sound of the waves.

The coast from Greystones to Wicklow town is a pleasantly lonely spot, remote from roads and devoid of seaside crowds. This satisfying state is explained by the nature of the shore: a shingle

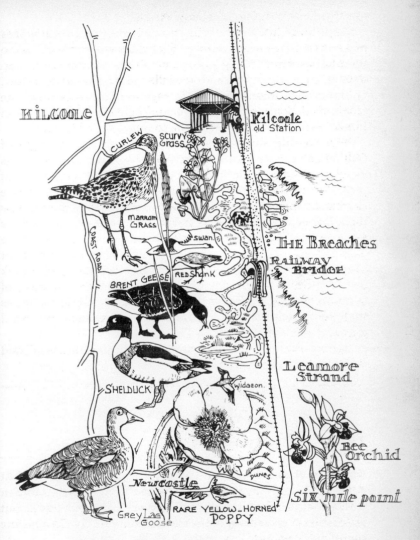

KILCOOLE

Kilcoole
old Station

CURLEW

SCURVY
Grass

MARRAM
GRASS

COAST ROAD

swan.

The Breaches

RAILWAY
BRIDGE

BRENT GEESE   REDShank

Leamore
Strand

SHELDUCK

Widgeon.

Bee
Orchid

Newcastle

dunes

Six mile point

GREY LAG
Goose

RARE YELLOW-HORNED
POPPY

The Breaches

beach nearly 20 km long. Several roads lead down to it, all of them ending abruptly at the railway line which runs close to the shore. One such brings you to where there once stood the railway station of Kilcoole.

A bronze plaque on a stone recounts the tale of the Kilcoole gun-running of August 22nd, 1914: a tribute, if any were needed, to the loneliness of the spot. The plaque could do with a polish, the salt-laden air having tarnished the metal so that the inscription is now a pleasing green colour and almost illegible. There you cross the railway line and turn right to walk along a level path at the top of a low sand dune.

In springtime, the sand is bright with the little white flowers of scurvy grass, a small seaside herb with dark green, rather fleshy leaves. It was an invaluable plant in the days before the properties of lime-juice were discovered and was a well-known antiscorbutic.

The railway was opened in 1855 and runs without a gradient for 15 km, the longest level in Ireland. Along the seaward side of the line a slightly disordered string of concrete blocks stands above the shingle. Each one is about two metres long and they are joined together by chains. Their function is to protect the beach from erosion and their effectiveness may be judged by reading the dates which have been marked on them in large figures. The top row was placed there in 1975 and the lowest visible specimens bear the date 1928. The recent blocks are in reasonably neat lines, but the older ones have subsided and been pushed about as the sea has attempted to carry away the shore.

The distant view is of the Sugarloaves, Bray Head and Wicklow Head, with Lambay to the far north. All the underlying rocks at Kilcoole are extremely ancient slates and shales of Cambrian age but the pebbles on the beach are mainly of Carboniferous limestone, a couple of hundreds of millions of years younger. They were carried from north of the Wicklow Mountains by the glacier which flowed southwards in the Irish Sea basin. Amongst the limestone pebbles there are occasional pieces of granite, purplish sandstones and small brown flints. The flints come all the way from County Antrim.

Down by the tideline patient anglers with immensely long

rods cast their bait far out beyond the turf. They catch the codling which, winter and summer, come close in to the shore.

Above the shingle beach, just enough blown sand accumulates to allow marram grass to grow and form a sort of dune. The proper development of the top of the dune has been prevented by pedestrians, joggers and dogs who together have flattened the ridge into a very pleasant, broad footpath, much easier walking than the shingle and safer than the railway line.

Behind the shore lies a marvellous flat area, up to half a mile wide, of slightly marshy ground, divided up by broad channels. Drainage operations allow the ground to dry out sufficiently in summer to provide a rich, green sward where sheep and cattle graze. Periodical flooding, however, makes it impossible to grow trees or hedges or to build roads so that the region remains a haven for geese, swans, duck and wading birds.

In winter wigeon and several species of wild geese abound and in summer redshank, oystercatcher and curlew all breed. In spring and autumn avid ornithologists prowl the shore because it is an important landfall for birds migrating across the Irish Sea and a good place for rarities when strong winds are blowing from the east.

A walk of a mile takes you to the Breaches, the point where the several rivers which flow from the hills into the marsh enter the sea under a railway bridge. Heavy seas in winter often move the shingle so that it blocks the breach and then the whole marsh is transformed to a lake which remains until the sea subsides and the impounded water can push the shingle aside again.

If you have taken the bus to Kilcoole you can continue the walk past the Breaches to Six Mile Point and find another bus at Newcastle, just a mile from the shore. Otherwise you must retrace your steps. All through the summer the dunes and shingle are bright with wild flowers: orchids and vetches and the rare yellow-horned poppy in profusion. Choose a fine day: there is no shelter on the way.

15 WICKLOW HEAD

Cars can be parked close to the lifeboat station at the end of the harbour road. Cliffs are relatively low and safe, but abundance of sheep requires dogs to be under control.

Silvery grey shaley rocks dipping towards the sea form the great promontory of Wicklow. On its northern flank, the Vartry river enters the sea, forming a perfect harbour sheltered from south and west. It was a natural place for the Vikings to establish a port, and ancient documents give it the name of 'Wykyngglo', corrupted in the course of time to Wicklow.

Maurice Fitzgerald built a castle above the harbour in 1178 and the site is still marked by remnants of ruined walls. A path leads over springy turf along the low cliffs for about two miles to the collection of lighthouses on Wicklow Head.

Beside the castle, the land has been laid out as a park, embellished by a collection of cannons. Some of them bear monograms of Queen Victoria and two are engraved with the date 1862. A little to the south of the main collection is a breach-loader and gun emplacements from the first World War.

The sea to the north of the castle is busily undermining the steeply dipping rocks, burrowing in to make caves with sloping roofs. Just offshore a group of rock stacks stands out. They mark the outer walls of a cave whose roof has long since collapsed. As you stand near the castle you may hear a muffled, deep throated roar down below where the waves are pounding within the next cave.

In spring the turf is bright with the white flowers of scurvy grass. A source of Vitamin C, its properties have been recognised at least since the 18th century, by which time its name was well established. John Rutty wrote in 1772 that scurvy grass 'is eaten with the colder salad herbs as Lettuce, purslain, etc.'

The path leads southwards beside the golf links and from a few hundred yards along it you may look back for the best view of the castle. Two corners are all that remain, standing at the edge of a massive rock which slopes steeply to the sea. In the distance are the Sugarloaves and Bray Head. The rock of Wicklow is Ordovician, between 400 and 500 million years old. Its formation on the Head leads to the low cliffs and series of small coves with caves which continue all the way along. At the next promontory, a cave has been completely cut through to form an arch.

The spring flowers, besides primroses and violets, include the little blue seaside species called squill. It is very near the most southerly part of its range in Ireland here. For some reason of climate, it is unknown in Wexford or the south coast.

Bride's Head, half a mile farther on, is a remarkable place. A deep cleft in the rock separates the head from the mainland. The cleft is about ten yards wide and thirty feet or so in height. It would not be so remarkable if it were at sea level, but the floor stands well above the reach of the waves and has a pleasant, grassy covering. It must have been cut off when the sea level was considerably higher.

At the eastern end of the floor of the defile there is a low stone wall, all that remains of a chapel of penal times. Beside it stands a lime kiln built of large granite boulders. The soil derived from the Ordovician rocks is deficient in lime, but the beach pebbles are mainly limestone, brought from the north by the Irish Sea glacier. The pebbles were burned in the kiln to make quicklime. This was put out in heaps round about so that the rain could 'slake' it and make it safe to use on the land.

South of Bride's Head the cliffs rise and become high enough for seabirds to nest in safety. Fulmars are the commonest species. The bird cliffs lead to the three lighthouses which form a turning point on the route. Two of them stand well back from the cliff and have been abandoned. The third is hidden from the landward side and a notice says that you should apply to the Commissioners of Irish Lights if you wish to enter the area.

An access road to the lighthouses makes a quicker, but less interesting, route back to the castle. It brings you past an abandoned farmstead, between pleasing banks of gorse and hedges of hawthorn to the main road.

---

16   HELLFIRE CLUB

Bus 47 to Ballyboden leaves you 4 km from Hellfire Car Park; follow signposts for Glencree from Rathfarnham. Lovely woods free from sheep and cliffs.

Speaker Connolly, about the year 1725, had a summer house built on the Dublin skyline. Strong tradition tells of its occupation by the Hellfire Club, even though that organisation was more inclined to use less remote premises near Dublin Castle. Whatever the true history of unseemly doings, the name now is firmly attached both to building and mountain.

The site was chosen with considerable care. It is not actually on the summit of the hill, but it does appear to be there when viewed from the city. It was built to be admired by the citizens and also to give an incomparable view from Dublin Bay to Phoenix Park and beyond. Before the end of the 19th century it was derelict and the cut stone had been removed to build a house lower down the hill. Recent years have seen a very satisfying piece of restoration work which has included the building of a staircase to the upper floor.

55

The hill was afforested in the 1950s and, more recently, officially opened to the visitors who have been tramping up the slopes for generations. The starting point for the ascent is the car park on the right, 200 metres uphill from the restaurant which occupies the whitewashed stable yard of the demolished Kilakee House. Just inside the car park, a narrow path leads up the hill, beginning between a pair of young oak trees and plunging into a dark forest of Norway spruce.

This species is distinguished by its fronds, which can be grasped without discomfort. Amongst the spruces are quite a few oaks, apparently planted at the same time, but looking rather emaciated compared with the conifers which grow three times as fast. After passing a small grove of beeches on the left, you come to Sitka spruce whose leaves, in contrast to those of the Norwegian kind, are only too aptly described as needles.

After the second bend of the zig-zag path, a convocation of 21 large granite boulders stands. Four of them lean in a huddle to form a sub-committee. They seem to have been assembled by human agency, but whether in modern or megalithic times is far from clear. There are several undoubted dolmens within a few miles of this site, including one of the biggest in Ireland, unfortunately on private land.

Just up the hill from them a clearing has been made to accommodate overhead wires. The clearing has been planted with noble fir for Christmas trees, which can be harvested safely before they grow tall enough to impinge on the ESB. Beyond them are older firs, and then comes a crossroad where the footpath meets the forest road which you may follow for a while. It runs beside an old field boundary, marked by a crumbling stone wall and some splendid oaks and beeches, perhaps a hundred years of age.

The next bend brings the forest road southwards, away from Hellfire, to skirt around the shoulder of the hill. From its most southerly curve there is a view to distant mountains and, nearby, down into the secluded gorge of Piperstown. It is a dry valley nowadays, but once carried a raging torrent of meltwater from the great midland ice sheet. The forest on the shoulder is suffering from exposure to the southwesterly winds. Larches and firs have a lean and hungry look, bending up the hill, away from the wind.

There is a shallow pond on the right and the track just beyond it leads straight to Hellfire if you want to take a short cut. Or you can take the left fork of the forest road for a longer walk. The chosen route is the middle one, going back into the forest until you meet a T-junction where the right turn goes up the hill, between larch trees on a path which in autumn is covered by a golden carpet of fallen needles.

This path leads you straight to the rere of the old building and a grim and lonely pile it is, too. It is all too easy to believe the unauthenticated tales of unpleasant things done to unwilling persons by members of the club in its heyday. Apart from its diabolical associations, the building is a remarkable one. The fabric is entirely of mortared stone and floors and roof are made by almost anachronistic barrel vaulting. Whether this very strong structure was employed to resist the wind or the Wicklow men – or both – is uncertain.

Concentric mounds of earth with some granite kerbstones lie just behind the house. They are all that remains of a passage grave, demolished to provide building material. The front view of Hellfire is less gloomy and dungeon-like than the back and the panorama of the city and bay of Dublin is breathtaking. On a good day, the distant view goes as far as the Mountains of Mourne.

The path back to the car park leads straight down the hill, passing one fine monolith of granite, two metres high, on the way. The path has deep ruts, made by occasional streams which have carried away the finer material of the glacial till and left the stones. Most of them are sandstone, carried up the hill by the ice sheet from the midlands which covered Hellfire completely.

17   THREE ROCK

The Forestry car park lies off a cul de sac on the Ticknock Road. Public transport extends to Ballinteer or to Grange Road, the latter being a quarter of a mile nearer. The forest is safe for dogs and children.

Three Rock stands at the north-east corner of the Wicklow Mountains and gives a splendid view of a great deal of Ireland. Sometimes you can see a little bit of Wales as well. Three Rock isn't especially lofty, but it forms part of the skyline to the south of Dublin since the higher peaks are hidden behind it. The ascent makes a pleasant stroll for a winter Sunday afternoon.

The rather barren slopes were afforested in the 1950s and, more recently, the woods were opened with the provision of a well-surfaced road and plenty of car parking space. You can drive to near the highest point of the tarred road and leave the car on the legitimate side of the 'no parking' sign. Here a road surfaced with limestone chippings branches off for higher places. At sunset, you may see deer in the car park.

The trees at this point are Norway spruce, until quite recently the mainstay of the Christmas tree trade. The needles are rather short and soft, pleasant to stroke. The path lies in a cutting between banks of yellow-brown soil containing angular lumps of granite, the local rock, and some limestone. Three Rock is a *locus classicus* for deposits of material from the bed of the Irish Sea. The glacial till as high up as 345 metres contains fragments of sea shells. Don't bother to look for them: the fragments are very small and it took the 19th century geologist Maxwell Close several years to find enough to be worth writing about.

A little way up the hill you come to larch trees, bare of leaves in winter and growing on a carpet of green grass. The spruces, in contrast, allow practically no other plants to grow in the dark shade beneath them. Close to the larches there are Sitka spruces, distinguished by their blue-green and rather prickly fronds, not at all pleasing to grasp.

The first major landmark is the old shooting range, now used for exercising motorcycles, and giving a wide open space in the forest with a view to the nearest neighbouring mountain, Kilmashogue and, far to the north, towards the hills of the Dublin/Meath border country. Closer to hand lies the bright green sward of a golflinks, making a sharp contrast with the higher slopes. In winter these are brown, with the dead fronds of

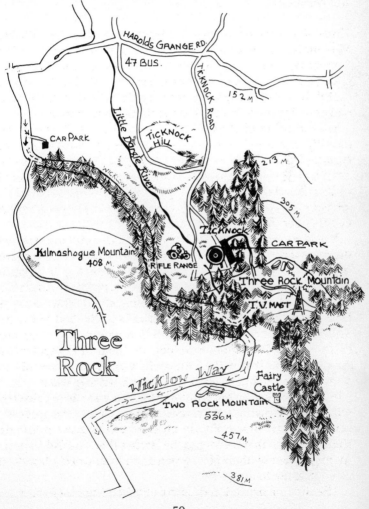

bracken and with heather. Even in summer, the green colouring is very much darker than the grasses lower down.

The grass grows on the glacial till which drains easily and has a high lime content. The lime is derived from the rocks to the north, carried by the ice sheet which travelled southwards over the Central Plain and through the Irish Sea basin during the Midlandian phase of the Ice Age, between 30,000 and 70,000 years ago. The Wicklow Mountains formed a barrier to the ice and forced it to deposit its load of stones around the lower slopes.

Beside the forest path the hill slope is being eroded by wind and rain, and trees fall from time to time. The deeper soil is decayed granite with a thin layer of peat at the top. The pre-forestry vegetation was mainly heather and gorse. The gorse still thrives by the sides of the paths, coming into flower as early as February.

The forest ends near the summit of Three Rock, the vigorous spruces giving way to windswept pines. The road leads to a noble array of radio antennae, pride of place going to the RTE 2 transmitter: a stocky pylon festooned with solid geometry.

The special feature of the top of the mountain is the group of granite tors: the rocks which give the mountain its name. According to G. F. Mitchell, these are the remnants of long-exposed mountain top whose granite was first rotted by wind and rain and further broken up by the alternate freezing and thawing of the water which percolated down through the crevices. In the course of time the shattered fragments were carried away, leaving nothing but the tors. Even they are broken up and consist in parts of immense loose boulders lying on the bed rock beneath. In common with the Sugarloaves and Bray Head, the summit of Three Rock stood out above the glaciers as a 'nunatak'. One more feature of the tors is the shelter they give to the mountain plants – as well as to mountaineers. Frochan, heather, bracken, wood sorrel and a variety of ferns all nestle into the crevices.

From Three Rock you can walk on to Two Rock or perhaps across to Kilmashogue. Otherwise the way back requires a simple retracing of your steps.

18 KELLY'S GLEN

Bus 47 for Tibradden has a stop at the bottom of Kilmashogue Lane. The walk goes through sheep pasture, and free-range dogs are most unwelcome, especially in spring at lambing time.

Kelly's Glen is the least remote of the valleys of the Dublin Mountains and yet one which remarkably few people visit. The crowds succumb to the blandishments of Kilmashogue Wood, its car park and winding forest paths. The valley below is left to the discerning few. It is a broad, open glen lying between Kilmashogue and Tibradden Mountain, closed off at its south-eastern end by the ridge of Two Rock. This is granite country, with smooth contours and gentle slopes.

Kilmashogue Wood is a relatively young plantation forming a belt of forest at about 200 metres on the northern and eastern slopes of the mountain. The car park lies off Kilmashogue Lane which climbs steeply from the crossroads above the church at Whitechurch, passing a watermill, derelict since the turn of the century. There are some old trees at the car park. They are Monterey pines, which look feathery because they have their needles in bunches of three or more instead of the two which are found in the more common pine trees. The younger trees are mostly Sitka spruce. Across the road stand sycamores and, on the near side, holly grows wild in the hedges, descended from bushes which lived in long-departed oak forests.

The land to the west of the road is gently sloping and fertile and enclosed by a mortared stone wall. The road itself forms a boundary between the fertile lands and the barren mountain soil. It was worth some landowner's while to build an expensive wall to preserve his stock while, to the west, the land was poor and has been provided with a much simpler boundary of large boulders devoid of mortar.

A little way up the hill, below four big sycamores, the boulder wall is exposed, its rocks covered with soft moss and with wild strawberries growing in the crevices. Just past the modern dwelling called 'Bracken', the uphill ground is strewn with lichen-covered boulders, part of the deposits of a mountain glacier. The fact that the boulders are large indicates that they have not been carried very far.

Higher up the hill is an old wood, with larches and Scots pines, distinguished by their beautiful orange-coloured bark. Across the road, after the second modern house, are the ruins of an ancient farmstead, the surviving wall neatly built of closely-fitted stones. Closed by is a pair of gate posts, each one a single piece of roughly hewn granite. Opposite the gate, broom bushes stand above the wall and the curious fern, polypody, with its oblong leaves and orange spores, grows a little farther down.

On the right there is a little grove of long-established European larch which bursts into leaf about the end of March and displays tiny pink female cones. The estate of Larch Hill down below, long institutionalised, is a busy boy scout establishment. On the left there is a further piece of forestry plantation, screened by Lawson cypress.

Kelly's Glen

Quite suddenly you pass out of the woodland to sheep pasture, almost devoid of trees with the exception of a scattering of windswept hawthorns. Bungalows have begun to sprout by the roadside but there yet remains one farm of respectable antiquity and, high up the hill, a stone-built sheep pen. The sheep pen has engulfed two old gate posts, massive ones built up from small stones in contrast to the monoliths lower down the road.

The public road comes to an end at the highest point of the route. There are traces of lazy beds to the right and, beyond them two tracks going through private property. One goes through a farmyard, while the other heads straight up the slope of Two Rock. Just beyond the stream there was a spa well, providing 'chalybeate' or iron-rich waters. Dr Rutty in 1757 had high praise for its medicinal qualities and it was bottled and sold to the citizens of Dublin for many years. The decaying building in the farmyard has cut stone pillars and seems to date from the great times of the spa.

Up the hill to the left of the public road the gorse and bracken give way to heather and a short climb takes you to the summit of Kilmashogue. The contrast in scenery from the top is very striking.

Kelly's Glen, behind, has all the atmosphere of a remote mountain fastness. In front you can not only see Dublin's fair city but you can actually hear the hum of its traffic. A walk downhill, towards the city, brings you to the Wicklow Way and so to the car park.

---

19   TIBRADDEN MOUNTAIN

Bus 47 terminus Rockbrook is 2 km from the car park. Approaching from Rathfarnham, turn left after crossing the bridge at the hairpin bend at the entrance to Glencullen valley.

A controversial tomb stands on top of Tibradden Mountain. An Early Bronze Age 'food vessel' buried with cremated bone was found there is 1849. The discoverers celebrated their find by building a neat passage grave on the spot. Whether this is a complete anachronism or whether they were improving on a structure which had been there before the excavation remains a mystery.

The northwestern slopes of Tibradden form a part of the Pine Forest and a car park, screened from outside view by woodland, gives easy access to a selection of footpaths. A notice tells that:

The planting of this area has been funded by the Irish American Cultural Institute as a gesture of friendship and support for Ireland.

Cars are contained by a barrier which you cross to follow a good path that wanders gently by the hillside. The land has always been poor: granite rock beneath and boulders in ice-borne gravel on top. The Midland glacier which deposited limestone gravel on the lower slopes failed to cover the mountain ridges and local glaciers spread acid till on the hilltops.

This meant hard times for the farmers but has been a blessing for beleagured Dubliners who are not welcome in the lowland pastures. Conifers are able to thrive on the poor soil, but the

many windblown trees show that even they have a problem. The uprooted trees have taken the soil with them and you can see that the roots were unable to penetrate deeply enough to gain a firm anchorage. In most cases, large slabs of granite lie beneath the thin soil cover.

Where the path forks, take the right turn which brings you back the way you came, but at a higher level, to a T-junction. The trees there are European larch, distinguished from the more common Japanese larch by their oblong cones. In spring the larch produce fresh green shoots and new cones with minute pink flowers.

Take the left turn at the T and a right turn when you come through a gate to a space where young spruces are growing. They have moved in to a clearing made some years earlier by storm damage to the older trees. The path is straight and narrow for a while until you come to the edge of the older forest and meet the heather moor of the higher slopes. The spot is marked by a mysterious barrier, made from three substantial posts with a horizontal bar. There is a seat nearby from which you may speculate on its origins.

A fire break, bulldozed through the peat, provides a path along the main ridge of Tibradden towards the summit. Along the edges of the path you can see where the peat has grown up between the boulders which formerly lay bare on the hillside. Where the fire break narrows and goes straight along the ridge, turn right for the path to the summit which is marked by a small cairn of stones beside the neat circle of the 19th century passage grave.

Whatever the date of the earliest tomb of Tibradden, genuine Passage Graves of the 3rd millennium BC stand on several of the mountain tops. On a very clear day it should be posible to see the great tomb of Newgrange: the bearing is just over the Papal cross in Phoenix Park. A little to the south of the cairn are several granite tors. Not quite as spectacular as those of Two Rock and Three Rock, these tors are remnants of higher layers of granite which were eroded by frost and rain.

Several possibilities present themselves at this stage. There is a long, but very pleasant walk along the ridges over Two Rock and Kilmashogue, back to the car park. The route marked goes steeply down the hill to the edge of the forest and follows this in a straight line. The flanks of the hill are mostly covered with heather but have great patches of granite boulders, occupying the steeper slopes. On the gentler slopes, in the course of the ten thousand years since the glaciers left, plants have grown amongst the boulders, died and decayed to form peat soil which has grown so that a smooth blanket covers the smaller rocks.

At the end of the straight line of trees, the way back to the car park is marked by a partly buried stone wall, one of the former field boundaries. This wall leads back to the broad path which gives a long and gentle descent. Alternatively you may go through the trees, straight down to the car park.

20   FAIRY CASTLE

Bus 47 for Tibradden passes Kilmashogue Bridge from which you go up Kilmashogue Lane to the carpark of Kilmashogue Wood. The whole walk follows the Wicklow Way and is thoroughly signposted. It takes about an hour and a half, mostly uphill. Most of it is in Forestry property but there are sheep nearby.

Fairy Castle is the name of the cairn on the summit of Two Rock Mountain. As a castle it lacks something. But its reality as a passage grave, perhaps 4,500 years old, commanding a magnificent view of the sea, mountains and lowlands, makes it a worthy place of pilgrimage.

Any approach to Two Rock entails a longish walk, but the Wicklow Way provides convenient car parking and a fairly gentle ascent from the northern slopes of Kilmashogue. The walk begins in woodland of a rather unusual kind. The first trees are Monterey pine and the next ones are beeches, both relatively rare

For Fairy Castle walk refer to map for Three Rock.

in Irish forestry. In 1989 the beeches were being pruned at an age of about 35 years and with perhaps 60 years to go before being harvested.

A Wicklow Way sign points along the main forestry road which you follow between the trees for the first 2 km of the journey. A clearing to the left of the path gives a view down the slope over the close-cropped sheep pasture and the green turf of Stackstown Golf Links. The forest edge roughly follows the boundary of lime-rich till from the Irish Sea glacier which covers the lower hill slopes.

Holly trees and mountain ash grow among the confiers, especially at the edges of the path where there is less shade. Both are taking advantage of the shelter from the wind and of the absence of grazing sheep which the forestry plantation affords. In autumn the beautiful golden rod blooms, a slender plant with bright yellow flowers. It grows in gravelly places on Howth Head and in the mountains, but nowhere else in Co. Dublin.

Where the hillside has been cut away to make room for the forest road, banks of glacial till are exposed. It contains many large lumps of granite, this is the local bedrock and has not been carried very far. But if you look closely you can find pebbles of greywacke and limestone and occasionally of blue porphyry: an igneous rock speckled with whitish crystals. These have all been carried from the sea bed by the southward-flowing ice field which filled the Irish Sea and covered the plains of the midlands. The porphyry was scraped up somewhere close to Lambay.

The road, after proceeding by gentle curves, begins to zig-zag as it seeks higher ground. Halfway up the zig-zag, gravel from the hill slope has been quarried to spread on the road. The Quarry is remarkably deep, about 6 metres, and has granite boulders of all shapes and sizes buried in it. Over most parts of the hill the soil is shallow and the pit is a striking exception. Here the gravel is composed almost entirely of granite, without any trace of the Irish Sea material. It may have been deposited by a local mountain glacier after the great icefield had receded.

At a half-buried gateway, marked by a pair of neat granite posts with pointed tops, the Wicklow Way leaves the gentle slope and takes a right turn going steeply uphill by a path which doubles as a stream in wet weather. This leads to near the top of the ridge between Kilmashogue and Two Rock, and you turn left to follow an old fire break. The going is a little damper, and the side of the path is bordered by soft cushions of bright green *Polytrichum* moss. Up here pines take over from the spruces and, with luck, you may see crossbills, rare finches which feed on pine cones. The males are coloured a vivid pinkish red.

Two Wicklow Way signposts come close together when you approach the nearest of the radio masts. The second one points to a scarcely visible muddy track through the peat. This is the direct route to Fairy Castle. A slightly longer way follows the wider path and gives a wonderful view over the Vale of Shanganagh and the Sugarloaves. Leave the path to cross the heather to the first tor on the right and then go back to the little pointed cairn on the horizon.

This cairn, a heap of stones, rearranged by generations of mountaineers, stands on top of the Fairy Castle. Beside it there is a concrete pillar, marking a triangulation point of the Ordnance Survey. Surveyors and passage grave builders both share a great yearning for distant prospects. From the cairn you can make out the circle of the passage grave, about one hundred metres in circumference and with traces of kerbstones on the northwestern slope.

The Passage Grave builders liked hilltops which looked down over fertile land. You needed a well-fed community to have the time to spare to organise the building. It may just be coincidence, but they may also have wanted to have their graves in sight of one another. From Two Rock you can see the Seefin and Hellfire Club sites and on a clear day it should be possible to make out Fourknocks and the great tombs of the Boyne, far to the north across the plain.

The simplest way back to the car park is to retrace your steps over the Wicklow Way path. On the way down you can see the green saddle between the brown tops of Kilmashogue and Two Rock which marks the highest point reached by the Irish Sea ice. After you reach the zig-zag, a track to the left a little way past the gravel quarry gives an alternative route to the main road.

21 TULLY CHURCH TO HERONFORD

Bus No. 45 serves Cabinteely and Loughlinstown. A very safe, gentle walk along a road with very little traffic. No sheep, but lots of resident dogs.

Within a mile of the teeming traffic or the Bray Road lies one of the loveliest of country lanes together with the peaceful ruins of an almost forgotten monastery. The view to the east from its high cross is of the road and the sprawling, if expensive, suburb of Ballybrack while to the west there are rolling fields of barley backed by distant hills.

You approach Tully Church by turning south-east at the traffic lights in Cabinteely and going along Brennanstown Road. Half a mile from Cabinteely a signpost to 'Tully Church and Cross' leads along a leafy lane, past affluent homes to a piece of level ground with a cross on a plinth. This is a good place to park a car.

The cross is a well-proportioned one with the Celtic-style ring, unusual in having no trace of figure sculpture. However, it does have a hat in the form of a stone replica of a wooden church and on that basis it seems fair to give the cross an age of a thousand years or more.

A slightly battered cross stands in the field on the other side of the road. It bears the figure of a bishop on its east face and is later in date, perhaps 13th century. The old church at Tully was a large one for its time and has a wide chancel arch built, like all the structures and sculptures nearby, of granite. Within are several of the early Christian gravestones inscribed with geometrical designs which belong almost exclusively to this part of Dublin.

Between cross and churchyard there are two pairs of stone gateposts, each hewn from single pieces of granite. They were made within the last hundred years or so and the plinth of the old cross was built late in the 19th century. So, from the early gravestones to the plinth and adjacent stone walls, there is evidence of more than a thousand years of skilled craftsmanship in the granite of the region.

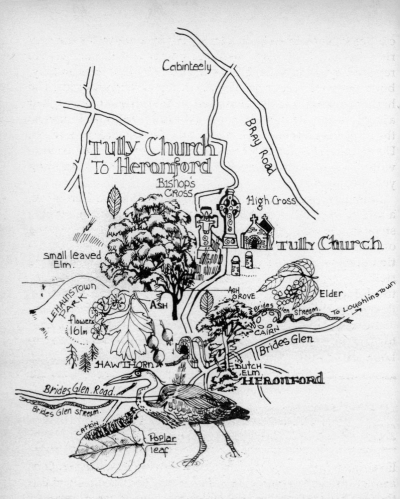

A little way past the old churchyard, the lane goes between modern gate posts. The tree above the right hand one is a rarity, a small-leaved elm. From this point you go between old hedges with hawthorn, blackthorn, wild rose and elder and trees of ash and sycamore. The path turns sharply to the right and passes by a grove of young ash and by more gateways with solid stone piers. Opposite the ash grove there used to be elms in the hedge until the Dutch disease overtook them.

Near the bottom of the hill is the gateway through which you can see Lehaunstown Park, a lovely old farmhouse. As the road rises beyond it, the land becomes poorer and the hedges are replaced by stone walls, hidden in places by brambles and ivy, but brightened occasionally by stonecrop and honeysuckle. The higher ground to the right has been planted with Douglas fir, but a large portion of this was destroyed by fire. The ground amongst the dead trees has been taken over by a dense jungle of bracken. Down the hill to the left, the scene is of pleasant open pasture with hedge, a dwelling for many song-birds, including yellowhammers.

From the forest, the road goes steeply downhill to Heronford, a ford of the bubbling Bride's Glen Stream, now spanned by a stone bridge with a well-made arch which you can see by leaning over the parapet. Herons do go there, though there is a suggestion that the name is really a corruption of Hearn's Ford. To the right of the bridge, aspens grow in a little swamp: delicate poplar trees whose round leaves tremble in the lightest breeze because their stalks are curiously flattened.

If you have travelled by bus to Cabinteely, you can return to town by turning left at the main road and walking about 2 km to Loughlinstown.

---

22   KATTY GOLLAGHER

Enniskerry bus 44 goes past Barnaslingan Lane giving a walk of a mile and a half to the Carrigcollogan car park. The walk within the forest is safe for dogs and children provided care is taken to avoid abundant broken glass around the Leadmines chimney.

Carrickgollogan is the official name of the round-topped hill which stands beside the Leadmines chimney overlooking the lowlands of south Dublin. The unofficial, but much more widely used name is Katty Gollagher, and in my family it was known as the Top of the World because of the wonderful view of harbours and hills and houses far below.

It is a hill with an interesting geological history. Having originally been part of the main mass of Bray Head it was thrust to the north and is now isolated from its parent rock. In the Ice Age, Katty's head and shoulders were left bare by the glaciers so that they were not covered with the lime-rich till which has discreetly clothed her flanks. What this means to her latter-day lovers is that the soil on the hillside is too poor for profitable farming and has been afforested. The Forest Service has provided a number of car parks and footpaths.

The best approach to the hill from Dublin is to travel on the Enniskerry road. Leave this by a left turn at the granite-built Kilternan Post Office to follow Barnaslingan Lane towards the Leadmines and park your car at Carrickgollogan Wood. The single path from this car park leads eastwards between pine trees which were felled in the 1980s at 30 years of age. Farther along, the pines are replaced by larches and noble firs with some oaks and Lawson cypresses along the sides of the path. In places there are large boulders of schist, grey, shiny flakey rock from the margins of the Wicklow granite.

The wide path stops abruptly at the steep slope where the rock changes from slate to quartzite. The quartzite forms scree slopes and small cliffs with bracken growing in the lower parts and luxuriant bushes of heather higher up. You can scramble straight up the scree slope, but a turn to the left leads to a narrow zig-zag path which gives a much easier climb to the summit.

The top of the hill comes rather as a surprise, being almost flat and covered with short grass, cropped close by rabbits. Towards the south, the contrast between the heather slopes and the lush green pastures of the lowlands is really striking. The distant view extends from the Mountains of Mourne down the coast over Dublin Bay to Bray Head, the Sugarloaves and Djouce.

The hilltop is a blustery place and when the wind is strong in summer, swallows beat their way upwards against it and then zoom downhill at a tremendous rate. Swifts and swallows often congregate on such isolated hilltops; possibly the local air currents bring an additional supply of insects.

Just down the hill, nestling into a hedge to the right of the transmission poles in a square green field, you can see a dolmen.

At the time it was built, four to five thousand years ago, there may have been dense forest where the pasture now lies and the site of the dolmen could mark the upper boundary of the forest.

Below the high tension lines on the hillside to the northeast of the summit, the ground has been kept free to make a straight path. A short climb over scree and heather brings you to it. This path goes beside an old stone boundary wall with trees on either side and occasional clumps of tall willow herb with pink flowers. Noble firs and pines for Christmas trees have been planted beneath the high lines.

As you go northwards the trees make a frame for a portion of the city of Dublin, the course of the Liffey being identified by red gasometers. Turn left at a crossing path which leads to the Leadmines chimney, built early in the 19th century. Built in 1862, it stands about 25 metres high, an elegant structure worthy of comparison with the round towers.

Lead was mined locally, near the top of the hill, during the first half of the 19th century. Ore was also brought to Ballycorus from Glendalough to the smelting works near the bottom of the hill. From the works, a wonderful stone-built flue winds its way up the hill to the chimney. The toxic fumes from the smelters were

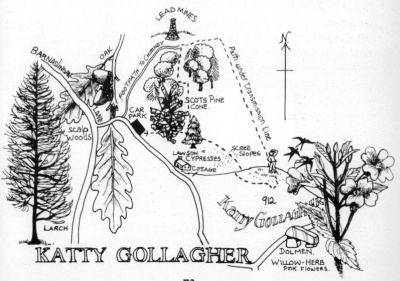

thereby wafted to comparative safety. Most of the solid particles in the fumes were deposited on the walls of the flue which were scraped down from time to time, after ventilation by means of the many doorways. Down the hill, to the left of the nearest group of houses is a shot tower. Lead shot was made by dropping the molten metal from the top of tower down into a bath of oil.

Opposite the chimney, a path leads down the hill along the side of the wood back to Murphy's Lane and the car park.

23   GREAT SUGARLOAF

Wicklow bus takes you to the entrance of the Glen of the Downs whence a steep road leads to the car park. The approach from the road to the west of the Sugarloaf is the easier for cars. The land is privately managed sheep pasture and not good for wayward dogs. The final slope is steep and stony but not unduly hazardous.

Great Sugarloaf is without doubt the most spectacular of the Wicklow Mountains. The steep-sided cone and the position on the outer edge of the mountain range give it a very distinguished look, in spite of being one of the lowest of the important peaks. Before modern methods of refining were developed, sugar was crystallised in conical moulds and turned out in the form of loaf sugar.

The rock of the Sugarloaves is the most ancient in the region, of Cambrian age and over 530 million years old. Much of it is relatively soft slate, but in places there are masses of exceptionally hard quartzite which forms the highest points. The quartzite is derived from the sand of clean beaches while the slate originally formed the bed of one or more muddy estuaries or lagoons. The same juxtaposition of sand and mud can be seen to this day on the coasts of Dublin and Wicklow, half a billion years later.

The conical shape of the Sugarloaf is explained by the fact that while ice sheets were covering and smoothing the hills to the west, it stood out and was exposed to the action of alternating frost and sun which shattered the rock.

The first time I ever climbed Great Sugarloaf I took a bus to Enniskerry and walked the rest of the way. But that was a long time ago and now I prefer to drive to the car park on the shoulder between the mountain and the Calary plateau. From that point a walk on a well-worn path for less than a mile brings you to the summit two hundred metres above.

The ground for the first part of the climb is sheep pasture on the left with tillage to the right. The underlying rock here is slate

which outcrops in places to trip the inappropriately shod. Gorse invades the drier slopes and in places there are parallel ridges on the ground, traces of lazy beds from former cultivation.

About the 350 metre contour, the ascent becomes less steep and there is a stretch of almost level ground. From this point, the heather begins to increase and the scene changes from one of gorse with little clumps of heather to heather with little prickly cushions of gorse. As you climb higher and more steeply again, the gorse gives up altogether and heather reigns supreme: mostly pale-flowered ling, but with a fair amount of the deeper purple bell heather.

The stones of the scree slope look black because they are encrusted with greyish-black lichen, relieved in places by blue-green and yellow-green species. Where the stones have been turned over by climbers on the path they show their yellowish-brown colour. The path itself is barren but, between the scree stones beside it, heather, grasses and cushions of moss grow and at the summit small frochan bushes somehow survive the harsh conditions.

The view from the pinnacle of the Sugarloaf is incomparable. In the middle distance to the north is the shell of Powerscourt House with its gardens which were designed to use the mountain as a backdrop. You can also see the top of Powerscourt waterfall appearing over the ridge of Long Hill to the right of Djouce.

The large fields on the ridge between you and Knockree are interesting in showing the fairly recent agricultural development which feels that big is beautiful. On the poorer land the scene is the older one of smaller fields separated by hedges. An interesting newcomer to the landscape is the reservoir of Turlough Hill whose construction has flattened the top of the distant mountain to the left of the shoulder of Djouce.

On a clear day the distant views go to the Kingdom of Mourne to the north and the Welsh mountains to the east. Closer to hand are the plains of north Dublin and Meath and a marvellous sweep of coast from Skerries down to Wicklow Head.

24   DJOUCE MOUNTAIN

The Long Hill is approached from Dublin either by Enniskerry or by Kilmacanogue. The walk begins at the third forestry car park going southwards, but continues on private land with sheep.

The ascent of Djouce is one of the most rewarding in County Wicklow. At 727 metres, it is the highest peak on the eastern edge of the Wicklow Mountains and thus commands a view from the Kingdom of Mourne down to the Wexford coast and across the sea to Snowdonia. To the west you look down on many of the Wicklow hills and up to Tonelagee and Lugnaquilla.

Like the Great Sugarloaf, Djouce is strictly an amateur's mountain, devoid of steep climbs or soggy bogs. The complementary exertions of Mr. J. B. Malone and the Forest and Wildlife Service have provided signposts all the way from the southernmost car park on the Long Hill.

This car park contains a map of the region, with a number of routes marked on it, every one of them worth following. The Djouce climb sets off down the hill to the left of the signboard. The bluish trees at the car park are noble firs. Squirrels live amongst them, eat the seeds and litter the ground with stripped cones.

At the bottom of the hill you cross a small stream and pass by the southern end of the lakelet. The path to Djouce bears left and climbs gently through a dark forest of well-grown Sitka spruce. You take a rather muddy path between the trees for half a mile. Then turn off to the left opposite an open forest ride which gives a view of Great Sugarloaf.

A short walk takes you to the edge of the forest and out to a fire break running along an old boundary wall. The stones in the wall are mostly greenish or greyish slates. The rock of the lower ground down the hill is slate, but up the hill it becomes more and more of a schist, a slate which has been altered in its crystal structure and generally toughened by the heat of the granite below when this was in its molten state. So the schist stands out above

77

Djouce Mountain

Glencree

WICKLOW WAY

maulin

LING HEATHER

R. DARGLE

457 m

BRACKEN

WAR HILL 686 M

CROWBERRY

Badger Set

727 M

Djouce

610 m

POWERSCOURT DEER PARK

P

P

SITKA SPRUCE

CAR PARK

RESERVOIR

NOBLE FIRS

To ROUNDWOOD

LONG HILL

GREAT SUGARLOAF

FIR CONE

TO ENNISKERRY

the shale to form the spectacular slope of Djouce and its accompanying hills at the edge of the Wicklows.

The fire-break makes a good path up the hill to the shoulder where you meet the first of the Wicklow Way signposts. There you turn left and south-west along a path which has been worn in the heather. It climbs gently in the general direction of the summit of Djouce which stands beckoning you 2 km away and about 300 metres higher up.

The dominant plant on the slopes is ling heather, the kind with small, pale purple flowers. It has been burned in places in an attempt to allow grass to grow for the sheep. There are patches of grass and sheep do safely graze, but they must have a harsh struggle for existence. On the slope of War Hill, across the valley to the west, the principal plant is bracken, its bright green fronds contrasting with the brownish shades of the heather. When you reach the 500 metre contour look amongst the heather for the crowberry, a plant known only to intrepid mountaineers such as yourself. It resembles a heather but has yellow-green leaves.

78

Follow the Wicklow Way for some distance past the summit of Djouce in the interests of getting as high as possible on the gentle slope. Then turn right for a short, sharp climb to the top. With luck you may pass a badger's sett: a burrow rather larger than a rabbit's and distinguished by a mound of dried grasses at its entrance, the badger being a scrupulous housekeeper in the habit of changing its bedding regularly.

This last part of the climb is delightful, if steep, over a dense but short growth of heather which feels like a spring mattress and encourages lying down. Those who resist the temptation attain the summit and can find shelter from the wind in the lee of one of the row of tors. The view takes what little breath you have left.

---

25   THE ROYAL CANAL
AT BLANCHARDSTOWN

Bus 39 to Blanchardstown. Cars can park safely on the right immediately after crossing the bridge going north from Dublin on the Navan road. This stretch of canal is ideal for children, dogs and even canoes.

The Royal Canal ought never to have been built but, by the grace of God, it was. It seldom flourished as a commercial waterway and that is one of the reasons that it remains to this day a most delightful place for walking and fishing.

At Blanchardstown half the original Talbot Bridge survives and just upstream the water level rises through a pair of locks. The masonry is neatly-dressed limestone. It was probably quarried nearby, limestone of Carboniferous age being the underlying rock of most of the lowlands of Dublin.

The first part of this walk, between Talbot Bridge and Granard Bridge, is rather well trimmed with a concrete path and mown grass on the verges. The water is clear as crystal and, to judge by the abundance of fisherfolk, rich in fish life. The bait most of them use is bread and the fish sought is roach, a small silver species with red fins. The roach is a newcomer which has invaded the canal since the 1960s. None of the anglers plan to eat the fish and the experts are equipped with keep nets so that they can contemplate their entire catch at the end of the day and then let them go again.

Ash trees line the strip of land between the towpath and the railway line which runs beside the canal. Beyond them are elders, whose flowers are good for giving added flavour to gooseberry jam and whose purple berries can be made into one of the most delectable of home-made wines.

About half way between the two bridges butterbur, with big green leaves like rhubarb, grows on the bank and in the same place one of the rarest of the canal flowers can be seen. It is an outsize buttercup, rooted in the water close to the canal bank and standing about one metre high. Its name is greater spearwort and nowadays in County Dublin it is confined to the Royal Canal, although a little less rare in the 19th century when there were many more ditches and pools in the county.

Upstream of Granard Bridge the banks of the canal have been slightly less thoroughly tended and water plants and bushes gradually become more plentiful. The very tall grass by the

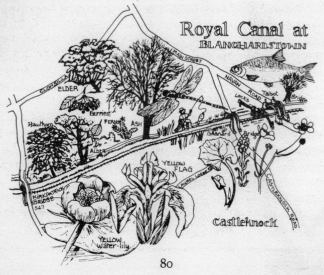

water's edge is reed canary grass while the water plant with pointed leaves which fringes the shallows is bur reed. In places there are beds of yellow iris. The beauty of the slightly unkempt canal lies in the variety of wild flowers, birds and insects which thrive there.

Down in the clear water in winter and spring you can see the submerged lettucey leaves of the yellow water lily. In summer its big round floating leaves cover the surface. Perch and roach, busily hunting for small insects and microscopic plants swim across the submerged leaves from time to time, showing up clearly against the pale background of the leaves and disappearing again as they pass above the mud.

The housing estate which occupies the far side of the canal comes to an end after about half a mile and from there onwards both banks are sheltered by tall, dark and handsome hedges. Hawthorn is the principal shrub along with elder, ash and alder while wild roses add sheets of pink and white to the greenery.

The canal continues to flow on the level, but the railway line rises and the towpath takes a middle way. The reason for the railway's ascent is that the rock surface begins to rise. This caused one of the most expensive operations in the construction of the canal – the cutting of a gorge in the limestone.

As the gorge deepens, the bushes on each side of the towpath grow taller and more dense and the way towards the next bridge becomes a covered passage, in a cool, leafy shade. In the more open parts of the cutting, oat grass and orchids grow on the shallow soil. Then the shade deepens once more and ferns take over the banks, especially hart's tongue, with its long, leathery, narrow leaves.

The appearance of new houses on the far bank and the shouts of children playing announce that you have come back to the world of today and to the next crossing, Kirkpatrick Bridge, built in 1795. You can walk on to the Shannon, but I turned and retraced my steps towards Blanchardstown.

This journey ends with a view of the green domes of Dunsink Observatory, perched on the edge of the fields which sweep gently down to the valley of the Tolka.

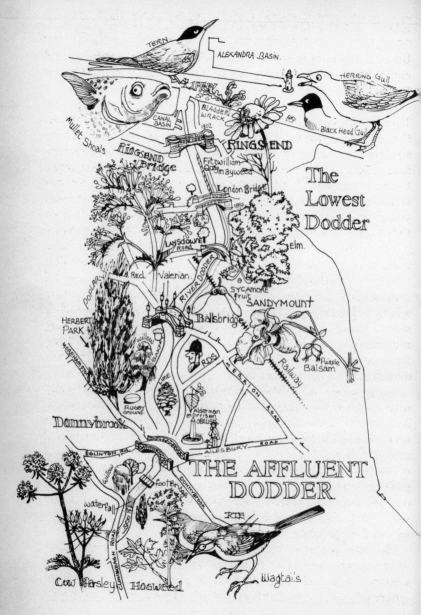

TERN

ALEXANDRA BASIN.

HERRING Gull

BLADDER WRACK

LIFFEY

CANAL BASIN

1802

Mullet Shoals

RINGSEND Bridge

RINGSEND

Black Head Gull

Fitzwilliam Quay mayweed

London Bridge

The Lowest Dodder

Elm.

POPLAR

Red Valerian

RIVER DODDER

SYCAMORE fruit

SANDYMOUNT

HERBERT PARK

Willow BRANCH

Ballsbridge

RDS

LIME

MERRION ROAD

Purple Balsam

Railway

Rugby Ground

Alderman Morrison OBELISK

Donnybrook

EGLINTON RD

AILESBURY ROAD

Willow

footbridge

DONNYBROOK

THE AFFLUENT DODDER

waterfall

CLONSKEAGH ROAD

RTE

Cow Parsley   Hogweed

Wagtail's

82

26 THE LOWEST DODDER

Buses 1, 2 or 3 to Ringsend Bridge. The walk is safe for dogs and children except for heavy traffic on Ringsend and Merrion Roads.

The Dodder is a sensible river. It rises on Kippure and reaches the sea after a journey of 24 km, in contrast to its unduly energetic sibling, the Liffey, which rises close by but embarks on a journey four times as long to reach the same point in Dublin Bay. Thanks to some inspired planning over the past century or so, you can walk nearly all the way along the Dodder. The lowest mile takes you from dockland to Ballsbridge by secluded footpaths known to few but the inhabitants of the neat, small houses by its banks.

The lowest bridge is also the most beautiful. Ringsend Bridge, built, according to Maurice Craig, by an unknown designer after a flood in 1802, has a single graceful arch and curved bastions, all in beautiful cut granite. Steps on the left bank lead to a quay from which you can see the Liffey, although you can't quite reach it since a house and a walled garden block your way. A surprising number of wild flowers grow there, the most conspicuous being the scentless mayweed, with big daisy flowers. An elder grows outside the garden and a poplar within.

At low tide the bed of the river is revealed as a mass of faintly unprepossessing but indubitably interesting estuarine mud. The brown seaweed, bladder wrack, festoons the stones of the quay below high water mark. It is a busy place, with much bird and fish life. Most of the birds are black-headed gulls, but cormorants and mallard, herring gulls and great black-backed gulls go there as well. In summer there are common terns, delicate white birds with swallow tails, which hover above the water and dive to snatch small, silvery fish. They nest on an artificial island close to Ringsend power station.

The most impressive creatures, however, are the grey mullet which may be seen in shoals in summer. Quite big fish, about the size of a small salmon, they feed or play close to the surface, where you can see them easily. One day I counted 141 in a shoal as they swam lazily hither and thither in the sun. Sometimes they rush about the place, often splashing and leaping.

On the upstream side of the Ringsend Road you must cross to the right bank where the footpath stays for the remainder of the journey. It begins at Fitzwilliam Quay, which has been built up in parts of stone blocks and in parts of concrete piles. The opposite bank is less firmly contained and mud and gravel are exposed to view. In times gone by this was a salt marsh or mud flat, but came to be reclaimed by the building of the South Wall in the latter half of the 18th century.

The next crossing of the river is at London Bridge, built, according to its inscription, in 1857. Upstream of it the influence of the tide is slightly less and a remarkable number of flowers and even trees have attached themselves to the upper part of the quay wall. Red valerian grows in profusion and then comes a line of sycamore, elder, alder and even elm.

Upstream of the trees the river takes a sharp turn and its character begins to change. The seaweed gives up, showing that the salinity of the water is low. A little way past the bridge, there are rapids where the water flows bright and clear over clean gravel instead of slowly and hazily over mud.

The final reach of the journey runs from the railway bridge to Ballsbridge. There is a great jungle of wild flowers on the river bank, the finest of them being balsam, with its big bulbous pink or purple flowers. It is an Asiatic plant which has run wild by Irish riversides in the course of the past sixty years or so. It is not even mentioned by Nathaniel Colgan in his 'Flora of the County Dublin' of 1904. The other dominant plant is butterbur or wild rhubarb, with its enormous green leaves.

Ballsbridge brings the footpath to an end and the character of the riverside changes abruptly from a secluded backwater to a scurrying world of traffic and busy people.

---

27 THE AFFLUENT DODDER

This is a walk for sedate citizens accompanied by dogs on leads. Although you can see and hear the river, this section is generally inaccessible for toy boats and paddling.

Between Clonskeagh and Ballsbridge the Dodder flows from bright green parkland, disappears for a moment into industrial squalor and emerges amongst the back gardens of expensive dwellings. Footpaths beneath tall trees allow you to stay close to the river for most of the way. The jungle of bushes on the banks makes a contrast with the neatly tended walks by the Grand Canal less than a mile away. With so much more cover, the Dodder is something of a wilderness, resounding with birdsong. Even kingfishers live there.

The left bank is the most approachable and the route begins at Ballsbridge, passing by young weeping willows and a very ancient poplar. Who the Ball of the bridge was seems likely to remain for ever shrouded in mystery. Even the historian Francis Elrington Ball was unable to provide much information on his namesake. All he could offer was a statement that a dwelling called Ball's House stood at the beginning of the 17th century on the left bank upstream of the present bridge.

The path lies between the bakery and the steep, muddy bank of the river. In 1989 a heavenly aroma of newly-baked bread still pervaded the area as it had done for generations. But in that fateful year the imminent demise of the institution of the Ballsbridge Bakery was announced.

Most of the trees are poplars, some old but with plenty of young, self seeded ones springing up between them. There is one fine willow and a number of elders. On the ground the banks are covered with butterbur, with its big rhubarb-leaves and with Alexanders, a popular culinary herb in the centuries before celery was discovered.

Immediately past the bakery, steps to the left lead down to a concrete path by the river bank while to the right there is a gateway to the lovely open spaces of Herbert Park. The left bank at this point is artificially built up, while the right has been left to itself and is lined with poplar, willow and sycamore. The lower branches of the willows are festooned with rags, deposited a metre of more above the normal water level by high floods.

The rugby football ground bars you from the river bank and you emerge briefly into the busy world of Donnybrook, relieved by copper beeches on the near side of the road and pink-flowering horse chestnuts in the garden of the Sisters of Charity on the far side. Lime trees line the footpath as you proceed towards Anglesea Bridge, built of limestone blocks in 1832. Crossing the bridge you walk along Beaver Row for a little, before regaining the left bank by an old iron footbridge which leads to one of the most pleasing parts of the walk.

The path runs beside a neat terrace between willows on the river bank and lime and plane trees on the footpath. At the end of the terrace there is a choice of ways. A muddy path goes through cow parsley, hogweed and other vegetation close to the water, while a tarmac path runs just above it. Both lead to the waterfall, the lowest on the river, made by a sill of limestone and enlarged by a milldam of lime-stone blocks.

The waterfall is one of the rather few outcrops of bedrock in the city of Dublin, most of it being hidden beneath glacial gravel or by river mud. The rock of the fall is slightly contorted so that it divides the water into many small, sparkling streams. A pair of grey wagtails live there, birds whose beauty belies their name. Their backs are grey but their breasts are bright lemon-yellow. They hunt for the flies which hatch from beneath the water.

Upstream of the falls, the water runs silent and deep. Once upon a time it fed a millrace whose sole memorial is a green-painted sluice gate on the left of the path. Before long you must leave the river once more, taking a flight of steps which leads to the Clonskeagh Road.

The return journey to Ballsbridge by the right bank keeps you away from the river for much of its length, but you can admire neat gardens instead. There is another milldam just opposite the entrance to Jefferson Smurfit on Beech Hill Road. Like the lower weir, it has been built at rapids formed by a limestone outcrop but here the rock is hidden away at the base of the dam.

At Anglesea Bridge you must not miss the inscription to the late Alderman Morrison. Among other distinctions, it tells that he was Respected and Esteemed. The obelisk is made of granite and surrounded by cotoneaster which provides berries for mistle thrushes to eat in winter.

The final stopping place is Ballsbridsge itself, where the coping to the right of the name plaque has a fine display of fossils, mainly the broken stems of crinoids or sea lilies – a reminder on cold days of the times when Dublin lay beneath the crystal clear waters of a coral sea.

28   UPPER LOUGH BRAY

The nearest bus stop is Rockbrook (47), seven miles away. Cars from the city go through Rathfarnham and Ballyboden, after which Glencree is signposted. Grazing sheep have prior rights.

Thousands of cars drive swiftly over the shoulder of Kippure on a fine Sunday. Fortunately, very few of them stop to disgorge their passengers for a walk to the shores of Upper Lough Bray which nestles into the base of the cliff. It is a marvellously dark and lonely lake where you can wander in stillness while traffic, inaudible and invisible rushes past less than a mile away.

As you drive up the road from Glencree, the lake appears down below on the right and, a little farther on, there is a quarry on the left where cars can be parked. The hills on all sides are of granite and the quarry probably supplied stone for the building of the road which began shortly after 1798. It is the highest rock outcrop on the path of the road and therefore permitted transport of the stone with a minimum of effort.

Across the road from the quarry, a path leads steeply downwards in the direction of the lake. Where it flattens out, there is a little patch of green grass making a contrast with the heather which is the dominant plant on both sides. The ground looks too poor and acid to support even this small piece of grassy sward.

UPPER LOUGH BRAY

Glencree

Knockmaun 555M Mt

Cemetery

Reconciliation Centre

Glencree River

Bell Heather

Lower Lough Bray

GROUSE

754 TV Mast

KIPPURE 685

UPPER LOUGH BRAY

CAR PARK

542M

610

533

542M Powerscourt Mountain

457

Liffey Hex Bridge

623

610 Tonduff 642 523

River Liffey

Source of River LIFFEY

BOG Cotton

Grouse House

Sphagnum moss

Grouse

Crockan Pond

Crowberry

CARRIGVORE 684M Mt

Sally Gap

WAR HILL 686 M

The Source of the Liffey

Beyond the green patch a clear stream tumbles down the hillside making a waterfall on the left and cutting away a small cliff on the far bank. The dark brown streak about 60 cm below the top of the bank is an 'iron pan', formed by the deposition of iron oxides leached from the gravel by water percolating downwards.

A well-worn path leads down to the lake shore, passing through a few soggy places and meeting the stream which drains the lake and flows down to the Glencree River. The lake water is very clear, with a slightly golden brown colour from the humic acids in solution. It is, of course, free from pollution but its clarity results more from the fact that there are no inflowing streams which would carry silt.

Visitors in the course of years have worn an easy path through the heather, just above the shore. This leads you quickly round a corner which cuts off all views of the outside world, leaving nothing to contemplate but water, cliffs and sky.

Lough Bray is a corrie lake, formed in the course of the final millennia of the Ice Age, when the destructive forces of freezing and thawing, aided and abetted by a local glacier, excavated a hollow at the base of the cliff. The spoil was piled up on the opposite side from the cliff and now forms a ridge on the eastern and nothern sides of the lake. At the northern end you can climb the ridge and admire the larger Lower Lough Bray with its lonely, but affluent, dwelling which has been marked on the Ordnance maps as "Lough Bray Cottage" ever since the First Edition of 1839.

The way back is along the top of the ridge. The ground is damper to the left and sedges replace some of the heather. About half way along you meet magnificent pyramid-shaped blocks which were collected and moved by the glacier. They may have been covered by the blanket of peat in the past. Some have little hats of peat with heather and patches of the same on their sides. The peat is being eroded on Kippure and there are deep gullies on the ridge where it has been carried away in wet weather. The climate nowadays is considerably drier than in the past when the same peat was growing.

29 THE SOURCE OF THE LIFFEY

The car park is 16 km from Ballyboden, following signposts for Glencree and Sally Gap. Walking is easy in dry weather but the earth becomes about as solid as a sponge after prolonged rain.

The birthplace of Dublin's river is a mysterious dark pool between the mountains of Tonduff and Kippure. Half a mile away, the busy Military Road takes cars unwittingly over Liffey Head Bridge and away from the haunting little glen. Everything is in miniature; the cliff above the pool is 3 metres high, the pool is 10 metres wide and Anna Liffey herself so narrow that you can bestride her. High above stand the peat hags and granite tors of Tonduff.

The Military Road is narrowish, but there is parking space at the entrance to the access road to the RTE transmitter. From there you walk half a mile down the road with turf diggings on either side and a little stream filled with dark green moss to the left.

At the bottom of the hill, Liffey Head Bridge spans the infant river. A discreet structure, its stone parapets barely rising above the roadside verge, the bridge proper consists of three concrete drainpipes perched one on top of the other. In dry weather the river is easily accommodated within the lowest of the three, but in flood she surges to a depth of nearly 2 metres.

The stream has cut deeply into the peat banks, leaving them 2 metres high on either side. Between them there is a flood plain, 10 metres across and covered by the beaten-down stems of rushes and sedges: dead and straw-coloured in winter, developing many shades of green in spring. The infant Liffey is a favourite haunt of the dipper, a little blackish bird with pure white breast which is able to walk below the surface of the stream as it hunts for insects.

In dry weather this level ground is firm and dry and pleasant to walk on but gets covered by a torrent when it's wet. About half way between the bridge and the Source there is an extraordinary little cavern in the peat bank: an almost circular hole with a clear water stream coming out and a little green fern growing at its mouth.

A little farther on you come to the dark pool at the base of a peat cliff in a tiny amphitheatre. This is the Source, the point where Anna Liffey appears abover the surface of the bog and stays there. The water in fact comes from much higher up the hill and you can see the tracks of two streams. Both of them, however, keep disappearing beneath the surface and flowing through gorges of runnels in the peat.

Above the dark pool there is a broad, open pond surrounded by a swamp of the pale green, feathery sphagnum moss. Sphagnum is one of the bog plants which, given the right climatic conditions, builds up into peat. At present, conditions are too dry and the bog is being eroded.

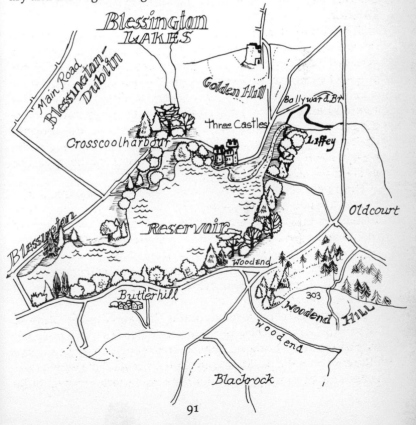

Follow either of the upper streams for half a mile or so to the top of the ridge. To the right a pillar stands on a hilltop, the last mortal remains of a building called the Grouse House. To the left is the summit of Tonduff South, the higher of a pair of peaks. The way to it is a gentle climb, passing through a wonderful land of dark bog and tiny, sparkling lakelets, the shallow ones carpeted with pale green mosses.

As you go higher, the ground becomes less damp and heather replaces the sedges of the bog. Sometimes there are bright green patches of frochan and, in places, little tufts of the glossy green leaves of the crowberry, a true mountain plant rarely found below 500 metres.

The summit of Tonduff is a marvellous place, marked by a great granite boulder carved by water into curious shapes. Nearby stands a mushroom-shaped tor. Nearly all the peat has been eroded, leaving a glistening white granite gravel interrupted only by tall dark peat hags. There are mountains in all directions: Carrigvore and Gravale, War Hill and Djouce, Maulin and Sugarloaf and the cliffs beetling above Lough Tay and Lough Bray.

The way back is a heavenly walk through springy heather where grouse rises up and sail away into the distance. The Kippure mast stands as a beacon to show the way.

30   THE BLESSINGTON LAKES

Bus 65 to Blessington whence a lakeside walk of 3 km takes you to Three Castles. The route gives half an hour of a brisk walk and is safe for dogs and children.

The Blessington Lakes look as if they belong there. And the forests that surround them blend perfectly with the mountain scenery. It is hard to believe that, up to a point, they are a recent artificial creation, owing as much to engineers, foresters and landscape planners as to nature.

The recent history is that the lakes were created in 1940 when the dam at Pollaphuca was built. The forests, mostly Sitka spruce and Japanese larch, began to be planted in 1959. Perhaps the most surprising fact is that the lakes are not as artificial as they seem. The Midlandian ice sheet for a long time formed a dam along the line of hills to the north and west of the lakes. This dam impounded an enormous area of water, extending from Brittas to Hollywood Glen. The lake varied in extent in the course of many thousands of years, eventually coming to occupy an area very much the same as the present day reservoir.

The ESB, owners of the adjoining land as well as the water, have provided easy access with car parking at nine 'amenity sites' around the lakes. All are marked on the map and this route describes one of my favourites, based on a castle and a haunt of wild geese. The ruin stands in the townland of Three Castles between lake and road 3 km northeast of Blessington. Military engagement is recorded in the State Papers of King Henry VIII for 1558 when an adjoining building was burned down. Its destruction may explain the broken walls which stand out on the south side of the ruin.

A path leads down from the main road, south of the castle, to the abandoned road which runs between banks and old hedges. These hedges are of great botanical interest in being allowed to grow in peace, safe from the savage attentions of mechanical hedge trimmers. Ash and elder are the dominant trees, together with hawthorn and wild rose.

Below the castle, the old road leads on through a larch wood planted in 1962, passing by snowberry and a horse chestnut, remnants of landscaping long years ago. The track ends abruptly at the water's edge, where the river is broad and silent at its entry to the lake. When the lake is very low you can wade across it here and it seems likely that the castle was originally built to command this ford.

At low levels of the water, there is a firm, stony beach by the lake margin. The stones are mainly limestone, carried up the hills by the Midlandian glacier at its greatest extent. A right turn leads down the river towards the lake where wildfowl are usually plentiful through the winter. Black-headed gulls, curlew, lapwing, mallard, teal and wigeon often gather in large flocks and in summer small numbers stay to breed.

But grey lag geese are the pride of the Blessington Lakes. The flock numbers several hundred and Three Castles is their favourite haunt. The month of March, after the end of the shooting season, is the best time to go and search for them. Also in winter, whooper swans often come to Three Castles. The only problem is that both geese and wild swans do go away from the lake to forage in the pasture round about so they can't be guaranteed.

The route follows the shore and turns right again to head back towards the castle. Depending on the height of the lake, the path leads over a sand flat or along the edge of a reed bed. This great plain of tall grasses is one of the habitats created by the flooding of the valley. It is almost uninterrupted, except by the growth of occasional willow trees. Pheasants live amongst the reeds and many small birds, linnets and redpolls among others, come to feed on the seeds. Hares and deer appear there from time to time.

The route ends more or less in a bed of nettles. This is a phenomenon as curious as it is unpleasing. Nettles fortunately will not grow just anywhere, they need plenty of nitrogen in the soil. Here they mark the site of an abandoned farm yard. Skirting the nettles leads safely back to the magnificent ash tree which grows between car park and castle.

---

31 THE FURRY GLEN IN PHOENIX PARK

For the Furry Glen route take a bus to Chapelizod Gate which is a mile to the southeast of the Glen. Cars find it by following the signposts for Knockmaroon Gate off the main road through the Park. Dogs must be discouraged from the pursuit of ducks and deer, otherwise a lovely place to exercise them.

Phoenix Park is a place of peace and beauty. Its small army of assiduous constables and groundsmen succeed in controlling the litter and keeping the grass trim, helped in the latter by the herd of fallow deer. The deer also browse on the shoots of the trees, as high as they can reach, so that the branches maintain a convenient height above the ground and allow you to walk beneath them.

There are many places to wander and a wide range of styles, from the People's Gardens for those who like their nature tamed, through the broad tree-lined avenues and the open space of the marvellous Fifteen Acres to the relatively unkempt Furry Glen which is the subject of this route. The park is part of the spoil heap of the great Midlandian ice sheet which crept southwards, scraping up, carrying and eventually dumping earth and soil derived from limestone. This glacial till is accordingly rich in lime so that a lovely sward of grass can develop. The ground also drains easily so that there are hardly any streams: just a few ponds, some filling hollows, others created by building dams.

The route begins at the car park at the edge of the Fifteen Acres, a quaint understatement naming several hundred acres of green sward where the deer often graze. This point is 500 metres above sea level and gives a view over the Liffey Valley and the industry of Clondalkin to the hills of Knockannavea and Slievenabawnoge and the deep cleft of Saggart. Nearby are fine trees, a little unusual by the standards of the Park, being of many varieties: oak, ash, lime and beech.

Across the road a little row of red-topped white posts indicates the head of the stairway which descends to the Furry Glen between plantations of pine: Scots to the right and lodgepole to the left, with hawthorn and blackberries in the middle.

At the bottom of the stairway you cross the road to the Furry Glen Pond. It was created by the building of the embankment which carries the road across the glen. But that happened so long ago that the pond has forgotten its artificial origins and natural vegetation has taken over completely. Water lilies grow near the edges and a jungle of flags and reeds lines the banks, providing cover for moorhens and coots to nest.

A footpath leads along the edge of the pond on its eastern side, lined by a row of tall, slender poplars. There is a pinewood to the right and across the pond a lovely wall of trees, sycamore and ash among others, which give a splendid display of colour in autumn.

The stream flowing down the glen carries silt which is gradually transforming the upper end of the pond to a swamp. Willows live and die there to form a little piece of wilderness in the midst of the well-ordered landscape.

The pinewood on the right gives way to an open slope where gorse grows. This is a remnant of the furze which gave the glen

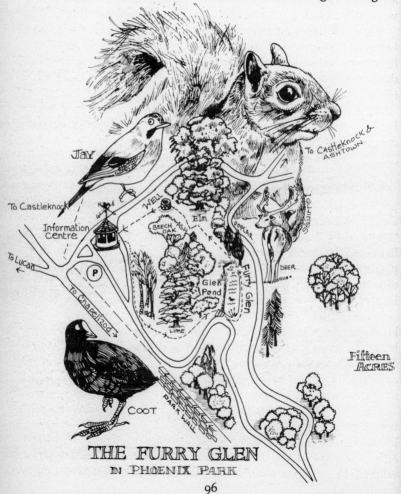

THE FURRY GLEN
IN PHOENIX PARK

its name before the tree plantations were established. At the top of the glen there is a little well of sparkling clear water, some of the 'fionn uisce' which was corrupted to give the Park its name. The well was roofed over with dressed limestone in 1894.

An arrow sign leads to the information centre which was set up in 1981. It is open in the mornings and afternoons and has an exhibition to describe the wildlife of the Park. You may buy for a modest sum a very attractive guide leaflet to the Nature Trail which this route follows in part.

From the information centre, a path runs over the grass between a pine wood to the left and birches to the right, leading from pines to beeches and so to a flight of steps going back to the dam of the pond. At the top of the steps are ancient ash trees and traces of elms killed by disease.

The route is a quick one, designed and executed within a lunch break. Many paths lead away from it, amongst the trees where deer and jays and maybe squirrels will be your companions.

---

32   HERBERT PARK

Buses 5, 6, 7 and 8, among others take you to Ballsbridge; the park is just to the west of the bridge and there is usually plenty of parking space. Dogs should be strictly controlled but can be let slip by the Dodder beyond the confines of the park.

Herbert Park is haunted by the shades of nursemaids and perambulators, toy sailing boats and scrubbed children. The park lives on, its superb flower beds and shrubberies as immaculately kept as ever, despite the passing of the nursemaids and their replacement by au pairs and jean-clad young.

The finest feature of the park used to be the lovely avenue of tall, slender trees which separated the athletic side from the leisure space centred on the pond. The trees were a rare variety of elm, *Ulmus sardiniensis* var *Wheatleyi* which were planted in 1909 when the area was laid out as a public park, after two years as the

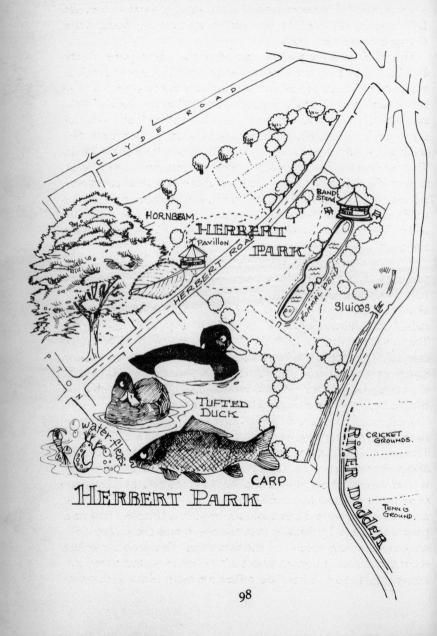

CLYDE ROAD

HORNBEAM

HERBERT PARK

PAVILION

HERBERT ROAD

BAND STAND

FORMAL POND

Sluices

PTON

TUFTED DUCK

water-fleas

CARP

HERBERT PARK

RIVER DODDER

CRICKET GROUNDS.

TENNIS GROUND.

site of an International Exhibition. Tragically the elms succumbed to disease and after heroic atempts to cure them had failed, were replaced in the spring of 1985 by hornbeams, *Carpinus betulis* var *pyramidalis*.

The wildlife of the park is centred on the formal pond. At the band stand end on the southern side there is a lovely patch of water lilies. These are all that remain of a notable collection of many lily species which were destroyed by the ducks. These destroyers, or their descendants, are alive and well and continuing to eat breadcrumbs when not grazing on exotic plants. The duck are mostly mallard, together with an assortment of hybrids. They are free to fly from park to park in Dublin and some of them nest on the islands in the pond. Some also succumb to occasional nocturnal foraging by foxes, the wildest members of the park's wildlife. In 1989 tufted duck could be seen on the ponds, part of a population explosion of this species which had begun to nest in the inner city a few years earlier.

On a sunny day at the southern end of the pond you will probably see the carp which were introduced in 1978: big, grey fish with a row of mirror-like scales along their backs. They swim slowly here and there, sometimes splashing at the surface. Carp need high water temperatures in June to succeed in spawning. This seldom happens in Ireland and populations of breeding carp are therefore rare. Herbert Park is one of the few places where they do raise young from time to time. Some members of the original stocking in 1978 were still there and very much alive in 1989, having grown to 12 pounds and more.

Patches of deep green plants, almost like clouds, bloom in summer beneath the surface in the less shaded parts of the pond. These are masses of microscopic threads of several species of algae. Sometimes you may also see pink clouds in the water which, looked at closely, have a fantastic appearance. They are planktonic crustaceans, often called 'water fleas'. There are myriads of individual animals, each about a millimetre long and propelling itself by leaping movements, hence the zoologically unacceptable application of the term 'flea'. The pergola at the southern end of the pond was built of left-overs following the International Exhibition. The pillars are built of the local limestone and shrouded with no fewer than five cultivars of the common ivy: they have to be expertly tended to prevent the plain green leaves of the ancestral plant from reasserting itself. The dome in the middle of the pergola is a new, Dublin Millennium one and is being rapidly approached by a vigorous *Polygonum aubertii*.

Making a selection of unusual things does only partial justice to Herbert Park. It is a most delightful place to walk amongst trees and birdsong, an extraordinary haven in the midst of urban traffic and office blocks.

33   BUSHY PARK

Bus 16 goes to the Pearse Brothers Bridge between Terenure and Rathfarnham. There is car parking space at the footbridge. Dogs are free to roam outside the park boundary on the river bank, but need control in the park. The walk around the ponds is about a mile.

Bushy Park is one of the happy accidents of nature which induced 19th century landowners to develop beautifully landscaped gardens. An even happier event for the plain people was the decision to preserve the demesne from the jaws of the speculative builder.

The Midlandian glacier filled the ancient valley of the River Dodder with lime-rich glacial till. In the course of time the river cut itself a new bed and formed a floodplain in the region of Rathfarnham. The banks on both sides of the floodplain are steep and would be easily eroded if they were not protected by the roots of trees and shrubs. At the bottom of the bank on the northern side of the river, the ground was swampy while, at the top, it was level and fertile.

The Shaw family (rich relations of George Bernard) who owned the demesne, used the fertile ground for pasture, but developed the intractable steep slopes as a garden and turned the swamp into a series of ponds. Since the estate became public property, one more pond was created and the level ground above was transformed from pasture to playing fields and lawns.

There are several points of entry to the park nowadays. One of the most attractive approaches is the footbridge over the Dodder, a little way downstream of Rathfarnham Shopping Centre. The park proper is separated from the river bank by a demesne wall of grey limestone. The stones contain bands of a black material: this is chert, chemically similar to flint and used by stone-age citizens to make tools. A concrete path runs between the wall and the river. Lying outside the park it has the advantage of being permanently accessible, even when the gates are locked for the night. Across the river from the path, where the bank is being eroded, you can see the glacial till: a yellowish brown clay with pebbles of various sizes embedded in it. Below it, the water runs around a mound of pebbles. These have stayed close to where they fell after the river had carried away the clay.

Following the path downstream brings you to a gate in the wall where a right turn leads to the new pond. The surroundings of this one are neat and clean with a tarmac path and paving to the edge, all inhibiting wild nature, if less liable to getting muddy. Compensation for the barren surrounds lies in the shrub-covered island and the fact that there is a dense growth of submerged water weed in the pond.

Thanks to this, an abundance of mallard, together with swans, black-headed gulls, moorhens and coots live there or come to visit. The coot is a newcomer to Rathfarnham. The closely related moorhens have been long established on the Dodder, but the river never provided the still, shallow water which is needed by coots.

The cliff above the ponds has a remarkable appearance, draped with a dense covering of climbing plants. Two species, bindweed and old man's beard, are responsible. Both of them start out from single roots and produce immensely long, trailing, leafy stems which invade bare ground and also envelop dead trees and branches. On steep, sunny slopes, sheltered from strong winds, they seem able to suppress all other kinds of plant life.

The path around the pond takes you to a waterfall and up to the higher ground, along by the tennis courts and beneath a splendid avenue of oak trees. Across the lawn from these, the ground dips again, plunging this time into a shady wood where beeches and chestnuts and a variety of other trees have been left to themselves for many years.

They surround two ponds whose surfaces are bright green with duckweed. This is an extraordinary plant, each individual consisting of one tiny leaf with a few transparent roots which hang in the water, never attaching the plant to the ground. The duckweed spreads itself thinly and is carried about on the surface by wind or currents.

When first laid out, this part of the demesne would have been bright and open and rather similar to the area around the new pond. Now the trees have grown up and keep the ground beneath so densely shaded that very few other plants are able to grow.

The walk through the park is terminated abruptly by a brick wall and the path turns back to bring you over a bridge and past a derelict summer house. It was decorated on the inside with sea shells, cockles and razor shells, probably collected from the shores of Dublin Bay. Close to the summer house, a gate in the outer wall takes you back to the riverside where you can turn right for a longer walk or left to regain the footbridge.

---

34   ST. ENDA'S

Bus 16 goes to Sarah Curran Avenue, a turning off Grange Road with a car park. Bus 47 at Whitechurch crossroads leaves you beside a pedestrian entrance. The walk around the woodland edge of the park is three quarters of a mile. A lovely playground for dogs and children.

'St Enda's School is situated in the healthiest, most beautiful and most romantic corner of south Co. Dublin'. So wrote P. H. Pearse in his school prospectus. The school died, but the grounds lived on and were bequeathed to the nation by Margaret Pearse in 1970. Since then, the estate has been made into a public park and the downstairs rooms of the house opened as a museum.

Pictures in the museum together with old maps show that little has changed in the layout of the grounds. In recent years the Office of Public Works has done an excellent job of tidying the estate and renovating the paths. Due respect has been paid to the old landscape so that the park preserves faithfully the whims of the Hudson and Woodbyrne families who owned it in the 19th and early 20th centuries.

Entry to the estate by the main gate is restricted to pedestrians, but cars may be parked within the grounds at the corner of the Sarah Curran Avenue. From the car park a path, bordered by young yew trees and *Tilia euchlora*, an uncommon species of lime, leads westwards to the Whitechurch Stream which runs near the boundary. Both species of trees are native to Ireland, a gentle reminder of the almost legendary significance of Pearse's school. Just to add to the romantic touch, Robert Emmet and Sarah Curran were guests in bygone days.

The shrub to the right where you meet the stream is snowberry, with small pink flowers which develop into round white fruits. It was a very popular species in 19th century country demesnes and has survived long after the original planting, often establishing itself as a wild bush. There is a choice at this point

St Enda's Park

of a smooth high road along the side of the playing fields or a more interesting lower one by the stream.

The low path runs through a riotous growth of cow parsley, butterbur and heliotrope and leads to a stone bridge beside an unusually tall alder. After crossing the stream by the stone bridge the path comes to a wooden one. The low left bank of the river just upstream of the bridge is a wall of large pebbles, set in a matrix of gravel and clay. This is glacial till, material carried southwards by the Irish Sea glacier. Most of the pebbles are of limestone, some are quartz and some granite. This mixture of all sizes of pebbles together with fine particles is evidence that the material was carried there by ice and not by water. Water-borne material is sorted into coarse and fine layers.

Stay on the left bank of the stream to come to the first major piece of landscaping on the route. William Woodbyrne early in the present century dammed the stream to make an ornamental lake and waterfall beside the crazy little castle. The lake islands have developed a wonderful jungle of willows and grasses and a fringe of yellow flags. Equally luxuriant vegetation, some wild, some descended from planted laurels, covers the southern shores of the lake. Such patches of wild plants are a rarity in suburban parks.

The lake islands provide safe nesting places for the mallard and the great variety of shrubs and trees in the park make it a wonderful sanctuary for small birds. All the common ones live in St. Enda's and it is a good place to look for such unusual species as goldcrest, siskin, redpoll and long-tailed tits. They are birds which move around the country a good deal so that their appearances are always a pleasant surprise.

The old woodland continues around the perimeter wall of the park and the path takes you beneath old trees and past the first of the antiquities which the Hudson family created in the 19th century, an erection of uncertain inspiration perched on a rock outcrop where the path rises to go over a ridge of granite. The park lies at the very edge of the Wicklow granite where this makes contact with metamorphic rock. This line of contact is often associated with dramatic scenery. At St Enda's you don't quite get a Powerscourt waterfall, but, true to type, the hills are steeper than elsewhere.

The path by the wall takes you past more of the Hudson follies, gothic arches, a dolmen and all sorts of less easily named creations and then through a thicket of yews to the main gate. From the gate you can walk along the broad, tree-lined avenue to the house with its museum and walled garden. The botanical highlight of the garden is the giant redwood. Most old estates have one or more redwoods, but few can boast of one with twin trunks. An injury early in the life of the tree caused two main stems to develop from just above the ground where the trunks are linked to form a giant letter 'U'.

Go in front of the house and past the outbuildings to the open lawn which runs outside the walled garden. On the left a collection of native trees, together with a selection of the most popular exotics, has been planted. The trees are little more than saplings at present and the arboretum will take many years to come into its own. Between the path and the garden wall a shrubbery is developing, native species again including gorse, hazel and holly.

The higher path above the stream goes beneath Monterey cypresses and pines where squirrels sometimes may be seen – Pearse wrote with deep affection of their ancestors. Obsessed with the need to bring young people into contact with nature, as well as with nationalism, he would be well pleased with the reincarnation of his school in the form of a park such as this.

---

35   MARLEY PARK

Bus 47b to Grange Road, well signposted from Ballyboden. Dogs must be leashed.

Marley Park is a triumph of amenity planning on the part of Dublin County Council. They acquired the private house and grounds in 1974 and have succeeded in preserving many of the best features of the old demesne while providing playing fields

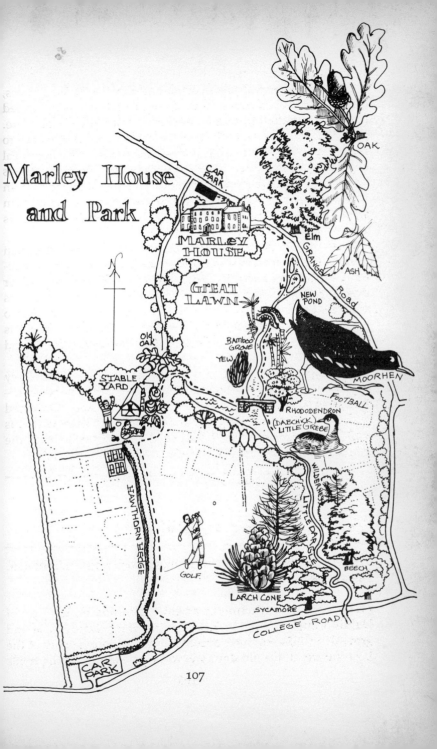

Marley House and Park

OAK

CAR PARK

MARLEY HOUSE

Elm

GRANGE Road

ASH

GREAT LAWN

NEW POND

N

Old OAK

Bamboo GROVE

YEW

MOORHEN

STABLE YARD

FOOTBALL

RHODODENDRON

(DABCHICK) LITTLE GREBE

WILDERNESS

LITTLE DART

HAWTHORN HEDGE

GOLF

LARCH CONE

SYCAMORE

BEECH

CAR PARK

COLLEGE ROAD

and a golf course for the benefit of the body and a complex of craft workshops for the improvement of the mind. The latter includes a tempting coffee shop.

The great house incorporates a more ancient mansion and was built by David LaTouche who bought the estate in 1764. His family were responsible for most of the landscaping which exists today, although tree planting had begun as early as the end of the 17th century when Thomas Taylor acquired the land.

The facilities include two car parks. That on the north side of the demesne is also the beginning of the Wicklow Way whose starting point is marked by a picture map of the nearer part of the route. However, the Wicklow Way makes a rather direct track through the park in search of, literally, higher things and our route is a gentle wandering one. It begins by turning left inside the gate to follow the wall for a short way to admire the old trees which make a border to the open fields within.

Most of the trees are mature specimens of well over 100 years of age. All of them are species such as oak, lime, beech and sycamore which have been long established in Irish estates. Such American trees as the giant redwood and the Monterey pine, imported in the latter half of the 19th century, are rare in Marley. There are more than five hundred varieties of trees and shrubs altogether.

The path crosses the Little Dargle stream which runs to a stone-arched bridge, neatly built of granite. The stream has been dammed to make a pond containing islands from which visitors are barred by water and by notices. Islands such as these provide safe nesting places for mallard and moorhen. Just upstream of the pond a new bridge has been built of concrete, delightfully concealed by more good stone-cutting.

Farther upstream, the Wicklow Way takes a right-handed curve to follow the edge of the great lawn. Our path crosses the stream to go beneath a shady canopy of tall beeches with an undergrowth of holly, laurel, rhododendrons and some yew trees. A little way above this, you meet a bamboo grove and then the first of the two ponds which were part of the original landscaping. Both have been formed by building stone dams in the stream to flood the low-lying ground nearby.

At the top of this pond, a bridge of brick and sandstone takes you back across the stream to the edge of the main pond, a lovely stretch of deep water surrounded by a beautiful collection of shrubs and small trees, copper beech and weeping willow among others, reflected in the still water. It is quite a busy bird pond with the ubiquitous mallard and moorhen but also having coot and dabchick, which are not at all common in County Dublin.

The path leads along the side of the pond, heading for the old farm buildings and passing by the greatest of the oaks. Then you come to the stable yard which has a beautiful rose garden in the centre and stables transformed to changing rooms for the athletic youth which inhabit the region.

From the yard you follow a wide green which runs between two old hedges, unusual in having been trimmed both sides but allowed to grow tall. Hawthorn is the dominant bush but there are many others, gorse, beech, holly and birch. This path goes past a marvellous open air model railway which functions on Saturday afternoons in summer.

You return to the northern car park by walking along the southern boundary of the demesne and then plunging into the wilderness which grows on both banks of the Little Dargle. The trees, larch, beech and sycamore, are youngish, less than fifty years of age. They have been allowed to take care of themselves and beneath them there is a lovely jungle of ferns and holly. Such a garden of natural vegetation is a rare thing in a public park and deserves careful preservation.

36 DALKEY AND KILLINEY HILLS

Bus No. 8 to Dalkey Village, walk up Dalkey Avenue to car park. Delightful playground for free-range dogs. Children love to climb the various monuments on Killiney Hill.

A substantial part of Dalkey Hill lies beneath the sea on the breakwaters of Dun Laoghaire Harbour. To appreciate the scale of the operation which brought it there you need to climb the hill and look down to the floor of the quarry more than thirty metres below. The thing at the top of the hill was a telegraph tower, placed there to make use of the astonishingly wide view which extended from Wicklow Head to Portrane and farther north.

Half a mile from the village of Dalkey, a car park has been made on the edge of the Hill. The route begins here, following gentle paths which have steps at all the steep bits. The region maintains a sense of gentility such as one would associate with the respectable townships nearby. The walk sets off through a wood of

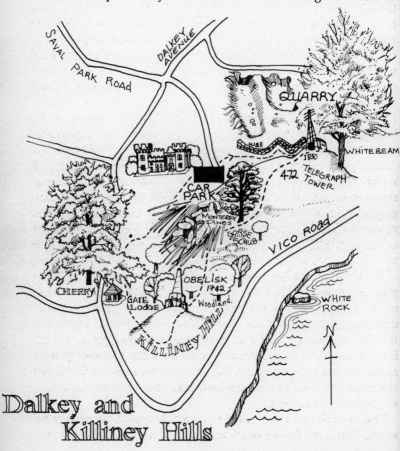

Dalkey and Killiney Hills

beech and spruce, which you abandon after a little while for gorse-covered slopes on the higher levels. A stone wall affords protection from the perils of the quarry below.

The soil is very shallow and in places solid granite rock breaks the surface, especially on the footpaths where any grass that may have grown has been worn away. The rock is smooth except where the surface is scored with narrow fissures. These are traces of veins of less resistant minerals which have been dissolved away by the rain.

Quite a number of trees and bushes have managed to establish themselves on the hilltop, in spite of the shortage of soil. The most interesting is a group of whitebeams, trees which are relatively rare in Dublin, although they are now being planted in increasing numbers in the suburbs. There are no old records of whitebeams on Dalkey Hill and these ones have probably grown from seeds brought by thrushes which had swallowed the red berries. The hawthorn which grows nearby would have arrived in the same way. Larches, ash and sycamore arrived as wind-born seeds but the presence of a single oak is not so easily explained.

The telegraph tower has been out of service for so long that it was already dilapidated by 1850 at which time Robert Warren restored it and placed a tablet of stone there to say so. A photograph taken in 1906 shows the tower still in an excellent state of repair. Dalkey Hill remains an important landmark and its summit is crowned by something resembling a trampoline which is an aid to aircraft navigation.

Walking downhill towards the obelisk on Killiney Hill you pass by the gorse scrub and then along the edge of a little forest of Monterey pines. Farther down and on the rising slope beyond, deciduous trees of various kinds grow where they can between the rocks. Killiney Hill still bears traces of the glacier which flowed over it twenty thousand years ago. The exposed granite rocks have been worn nearly flat on the upstream side but curve sharply downwards on the downstream. The formation is known as 'roches moutonnees'.

The obelisk was built in 1742 by John Mapas to provide relief work, 'last year being hard with the poor', according to his inscription. Like the signal tower nearby, the obelisk was also repaired by Robert Warren in the 19th century.

The railed-in structure near the obelisk, with its cotoneaster covering, is a water reservoir. From the hilltop the path follows a wall for some way and then reaches more woodland and a sadly boarded-up gate lodge. The trees here are bigger and more orderly than on the higher parts, but the park retains its friendly, unkempt feeling until you pass an exceptionally large cherry tree and emerge into the open.

---

37   SLIEVE THOUL

Bus 65 stops at Brittas. Signposts for Slade Valley golf club indicate the road which passes the Forestry car park. A gentle hill walk of 5 km, good for dogs and safe for children.

The view of Ireland from Slieve Thoul is an uncommonly fine one, making the gentle climb to its shoulders well worth the effort. Its position at the northwest corner of the Wicklow Mountains, rising straight up from the plain, makes it slightly invisible and almost unknown to devotees of the mountains who usually want to plunge into the remote fastnesses.

Also known as Saggart Hill, it is one of the low hills on the west of the main road to Blessington and has been the scene of forestry activities for more than fifty years. The whole top of the hill has been planted with conifers and a car park on the east side provides a safe stopping place off the exceedingly narrow and tortuous roads which encircle the forest. The taller trees around the car park are survivors of the original planting in 1934.

From the car park a straight avenue, bordered by birch trees, leads up the hill. Technically, the avenue is a 'ride', one of a number of straight, open pathways which divide the forest into separate compartments, each of fifty acres. The trees on the left with dark green, flat fronds are silver firs, planted in 1968, unusual trees in Irish forestry and a change from the ubiquitous

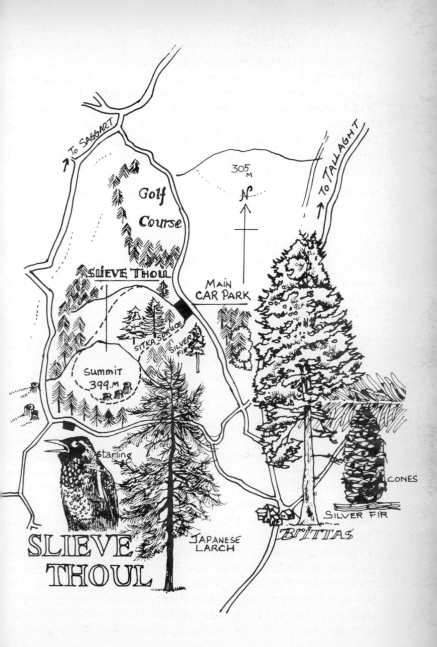

To SAGGART

Golf
Course

305 M

To TALLAGHT

N

SLIEVE THOUL

Main
CAR PARK

SITKA SPRUCE

SILVER FIR

Summit
399. M

Starling

CONES

SILVER FIR

SLIEVE
THOUL

JAPANESE
LARCH

BRITTAS

113

Sitka spruce which grows on the right.

About 50 metres up the hill, the ride crosses a roadway and continues upwards, though not so steeply. The tree at the corner on the left, across the road is a Japanese larch. The number painted on it, 36S, is the reference number of the compartment where it is growing. This larch is another veteran of the 1934 planting, which was something of a failure from the strictly commercial point of view. Slieve Thoul, at 300 metres, is too high for larches to grow in comfort.

Beyond the larches, the trees on the hilltop were felled in 1982 at the age of 47 years. There is an air of desolation in a forest clear-felled according to current ways of tree husbandry. On all sides the 'lop and top', dead branches and treetops, are left to decay in pathetic heaps of brown and grey brushwood. The reason for leaving the wreckage is that the natural decay gradually returns to the soil the chemical nutrients which would otherwise be removed and burned wastefully.

Follow the rather winding forest road through the clear-felling, towards the west. About half way across there is a luxuriant crop of nettles, quite out of place and of remarkable origin. In the 1960s immense numbers of starlings chose certain trees on Slieve Thoul for a roost in winter. They actually killed some of the trees and also deposited such large quantities of droppings that the ground has remained abnormally rich in nitrogen ever since and nitrogen is what nettles need.

Where the forest begins again, there are larches to the right and you can see a squirrel's drey high up on one of them, a rather untidy ball of twigs on a branch, tucked in close to the trunk.

The road comes out of the wood for a while, giving a marvellous view over the plains of Kildare and Meath. It then circles round the southern flank of the hill near the edge of the forest. The summit is crowned by a congregation of aerial masts. Most of them are used in private communications systems and have been placed there to benefit from the uninterrupted view over Dublin and the lowlands.

The path back to the car park passes by more open ground, with young noble firs on the right and, farther on, a jungle of gorse and birch which almost smother the young forestry trees.

Stones in the cut-away bank by the track are greenish grey greywackes of Ordovician age. They represent the old rock which was folded to form the Wicklow Mountains some 450 million years ago. The core of the folding lies in the higher mountains to the east where the greywackes are replaced by granite.

---

38   BALLINASCORNEY WOOD

Bus 49a stops about 3 km and 200 metres below the car park. The wood is fenced and contains stray sheep. The Forest Service has a notice requesting that dogs be led. Reasonably safe and full of adventurous climbs for children.

A miniature valley complete with lakelet and waterfall lies less than two hundred metres off the hill road from Bohernabreena to Brittas. It is so small that it is hidden from view by the elderly trees of Ballinascorney Wood. Even from the Forestry car park, lake and stream are invisible. Much of the wood was clear-felled in 1988, but a generous fringe of pine and larch was left along the roadside.

The wood stands on the lower slopes of Knockannavea Mountain, about a mile southwest of Ballinascorney Gap. It was planted quite a long time ago and is marked on the maps of the 1930s. The plantations of this period, before the days of the popularity of Sitka spruce, contain Norway spruce and Scots pine.

A walk down the hill from the car park in the direction of a group of four lonesome pines leads to a knoll from which you can view the valley. The lakelet is artificial and the water is much lower than in former times since the dam which contained it has been breached. A stream comes tumbling over the boulders into a broad, flat valley below.

It seems a curious place for a reservoir. The only large dwelling close by is Ballinascorney House, some way up the hill and therefore hardly in a position to benefit from the water. However, old maps show two houses down below and also a millrace. No traces of the houses remain and the millrace has fallen into decay.

The forest road takes you downhill to cross the stream by a bridge upstream of the lakelet. The stones on the bed of the stream are flat and black for the most part. The rock is greywacke of Ordovician age, older and more resistant than the Carboniferous limestone which forms the plain of Dublin to the north. The greywacke was laid down as a sediment on the floor of a former

ocean and then subjected to a long period of crumpling. During this time hundreds of sheets of an igneous rock, dolerite, were injected between the beds of the sediments. These intrusions are so numerous that they are described as a 'swarm' and can be traced by the dozen all the way from Saggart to the Hellfire Club.

The larger dolerite intrusions are being quarried for road metal. There are abandoned quarries to the north and a big, busy new one to the southwest. The rock itself outcrops to form mini-cliffs in the little gorge downstream of the dam. The dolerite was formed about 400 million years ago, some time before the nearby Wicklow granite.

Just beside the bridge stands a big block of dolerite, dumped by a passing glacier and generously shaped by nature to form a seat with a back to it. The valley upstream is especially beautiful in spring when golden saxifrage and primroses are in flower but the cut-over forest needs to be seen in summer when the foxgloves are in bloom.

From the bridge you take the right hand fork of the forest road uphill towards the edge of the wood. The road comes to an end in a small quarry, dug out from the glacial till which covers the ground here. The face of the quarry gives an intriguing profile of the history of long past events. The top layer is of stones embedded with clay – material which has been scooped up and carried by moving ice. Below this there is fine sand, deposited by a river of meltwater. Then comes another layer of glacial till and, still lower one more of water-borne 'outwash' gravel. Further down in the main valley the outwash gravel accumulated to such an extent that it has been quarried for years.

Follow a small side-valley up the hill to meet a branch of the forest road. This valley, like the main one, was carved out by meltwater: it is practically dry now and certainly could not have been excavated by the trickle which flows in wet weather. A left turn brings you back to the bridge, giving a glimpse of the secluded Ballinascorney House. If you are full of energy you might be tempted to take another branch of the forest road which goes up the hill in the direction of Seahan Mountain and its Passage Grave.

39 THE MASSY WOODS

Bus 47 goes to Rockbrook which is about 1 km from the estate (turn right along the cul de sac at the cemetery up the hill from Rockbrook). Cars follow signposts for Glencree. The woods are visited by occasional horses and riders and are secure and great fun for dogs and children.

From the Hellfire Club, the hill slopes steeply down to the valley of the Rockbrook Stream, passing through one of the most attractive woodland areas in Dublin. It was once the demesne of Kilakee House, the seat of Lord Massy until sold to the Land Commission in the 1930s by the impoverished 8th Baron. The estate was given over to forestry plantation but, from the start, it was a plantation with a difference. Broad-leaved trees, Spanish chestnut in particular, were planted instead of the usual conifers. They have now grown to a fair size and make a lovely place to walk in winter, over a carpet of crunchy fallen leaves.

Opposite to the entrance to Kilakee Arts and Crafts (where they serve teas, too) there is a car park at the top of a winding forest road which brings you down into the valley. The road carefully takes a zig-zag course to preserve a number of fine old trees, including an enormous sycamore whose branches are festooned at all times of the year with tufts of the fresh green leaves of polypody fern.

At the lowest point of the winding road you turn left and northwards along the next path which brings you first to an outlandish larch on the right, a big, old tree with a dense growth of thin, wispy branches. On the hillside to the left Spanish chestnuts grow. Tall, slender trees with grey bark and slightly woolly buds, they bear edible chestnuts in their native Spain. Here the weather is seldom warm enough to encourage the fruits to develop. Down the hill from the chestnuts, beech and some oak are growing.

If you leave the main path where it turns to go down the hill and head straight on, you come to the site of Kilakee House. It did not enjoy a long life, having been built in Victorian times only to

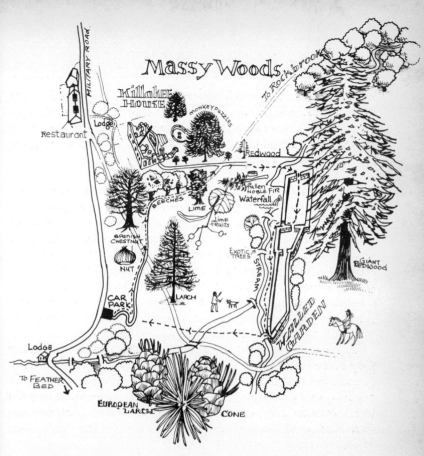

perish in the 1940s, abandoned and unloved. In 1988 a new house was built on the foundations of the old one.

The path going on down the hill passes a pair of monkey-puzzles on the left, the lowest members of the most unusual avenue of this species which ran down from beside the garden of the big house. The avenue may have gone farther down the hill and in any case points in the direction of the walled garden down on the floor of the valley. Following the line brings you to a grove of exotic trees, firs and pines and cypress.

From the grove the direct path to the garden is exceedingly slithery and it is easier to make your way through the woods to the right and so to the stream where it passes the bottom of the garden. The stone borders to the flower beds together with a series of terraces and broad steps remain to give a hint of ancient splendours. The circle of paving is all that remains of a glass house which is named on the 1843 Ordnance Survey map.

While the garden within the walls has been daintily planned, landscaping and tree planting on a grander scale marks the valley outside. A gateway in the wall at the top of the garden leads to more great trees, among them a redwood and a cryptomeria. The left bank of the stream is a small cliff of glacial gravel with enormous boulders of granite. Below them are some fallen boulders which look as if they may once have formed a footbridge.

A leafy path goes up the hill amongst laurels above the sparkling river. To the right you meet the first of two bridges, this one curiously constructed of a single span of eight hewn granite blocks, each about 4 metres long. Keep to the right bank, passing the ice house to reach the next bridge a little way upstream of a waterfall. This bridge is wider than the lower one and needed a central pier to support it. The ice house used to be packed with snow in winter and would keep cold for many months thereafter, permitting ice for drinks to be supplied and also used for storing food.

Cross the bridge and go through the gap in the laurels to find a sidestream flanked with big bunches of male fern – a sexless plant in spite of the name the herbalists gave it. Thereafter, a walk straight up the hill under the beech trees brings you back to the car park.

40   THE SCALP

Bus 44 stops in the Scalp. The route includes a descent unsuitable for perambulators and a short piece of main road with no refuge for wayward dogs.

The great rocky cleft of the Scalp is one of the most dramatic features of the scenery of Dublin and Wicklow. It shows up on the skyline from as far away as Phoenix Park. At close quarters the steep slopes, strewn with colossal angular boulders of granite, stand as a challenge to energetic climbers. We will ignore the challenge and take a gentle approach to the eastern summit.

The choice is either to take a bus to the Scalp and climb up by the lane which begins about 100 metres south of the bus stop or to drive to the Barnaslingan Wood car park where this route begins. Turn off the main Sandyford-Enniskerry road at the granite-faced Kilternan Post Office and follow Barnaslingan Lane.

The car park is on the right near the top of the hill. It has been pleasantly landscaped and planted with larch, birch and beech. The junction between Wicklow granite to the northwest and its aureole of schist to the southeast crosses the gorge at its southern end. The nearby hills visible from the wood are much older Cambrian strata dominated by the quartzite peaks of Sugarloaf and Katty Gollagher.

Just in front of a wooden stile stands a reception committee of young Douglas firs. They are easily identified by their cones which bear curious three-pointed bracts sticking out between the scales. A variety of trees has been planted by the forest paths: Monterey pines with big cones attached to the trunk, Scots pines with orange red bark and Corsican pines with smooth bark and long needles. Nearly half way to the summit the young trees to the right mark the spot where many older ones were blown down by storms.

A little to the west, the path meets an old field boundary, a low wall covered in flowers and with a good crop of frochans to the left. In spring they bear little pink, bell-shaped flowers, in autumn delectable blue-black berries.

Beyond the stone wall the great granite boulders which cover the steep slopes of the Scalp make their first appearance. There is a cluster of lodgepole pines and Scots pines growing amongst the boulders. As you approach the summit, the trees become fewer and fewer and gorse, broom and heather take over together with some small oaks and sapling mountain ash.

There is a good view from the summit and it includes, just to the right of the opposite side of the Scalp, the rather inaccessible and private woodland caled Ballybetagh. This is a place of profound importance in the understanding of the recent geological history of Ireland. It was famous in the 19th century as a rich source of the skeletons and especially the antlers of of the great Irish deer – those antlers which grace the halls of all the best country houses. Beginning in 1934, the sediments were studied in minute detail by Knud Jessen who, encouraged by R. Ll. Praeger and assisted by Frank Mitchell, laid the foundations of modern postglacial studies.

The descent of the Scalp is more suited to mountain goats than to sane humans, but it is great fun. Squirrels abound on the hillside: if you don't actually see them the evidence lies in the chewed up pine cones which litter the ground. The gorge was cut by a torrential river of which no trace now remains. The torrrent was of meltwater from snow and ice during the second last glaciation, the Munsterian, when, more than 130,000 years ago, the whole of Ireland was covered by an ice sheet.

At the bottom of the hill there is a gate with a muddy track to the left which leads past a morgue of motor cars to a marsh and an impenetrable tangle of brambles. The route is not recommended, even though it takes you past noble oaks and exceptionally fine old Norway spruces.

To the right there is a lovely path beginning after a short walk along the main road. The Forestry trees on both sides are giant fir, distinguished by its flat, almost fern-like fronds. The path takes a sharp bend at the 200 metre contour and ends abruptly at the foot of a silver birch. From this point the way upwards is easy and delightful, crunching over fallen leaves of beech and oak and mercifully free from brambles.

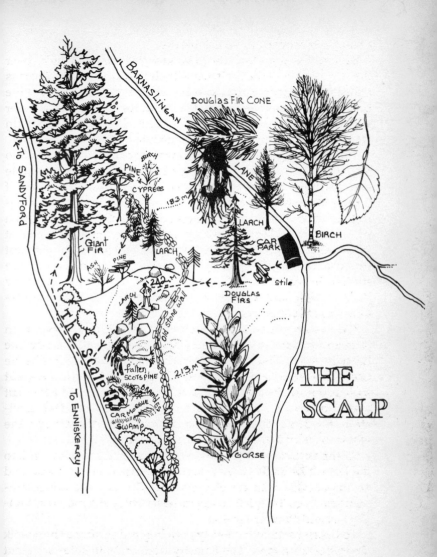

The return route simply heads for the summit, passing from forest to the open gorse and bracken with ravens and herring gulls soaring high above.

41 KNOCKSINK WOOD

Bus 44 goes to Enniskerry. Entrance to the wood is off the main road to the north of the church. Ideal spot for dogs and children.

Knocksink is a lovely, hidden wood close to the village of Enniskerry. A sharp U-bend in the valley brings you quickly out of sight of the busy world of cars and narrow roads and into a green-carpeted haven of bird song and a bright, clear burbling stream.

Cars can be driven half a mile into the wood to a car park down beside the river, passing first by a small forest of oak trees and a rather lonely Scots pine which looks poised to throw itself headlong down the cliff. The car park is guarded by two senior oaks, one leaning towards the river, the other standing stiffly erect.

The level ground there is just below the 100 metre contour and the sides of the valley rise steeply in all directions to about 150 metres. The river has cut its way down through a great mass of glacial till which once filled an older and larger valley cut in the rock. The many islands are composed of gravel containing small pieces of limestone and relatively large lumps of granite. The limestone was carried from far away by the Irish Sea ice while the granite is local.

A footpath goes upstream, keeping in a fairly straight line past the meanders. The floor of the valley and the hillsides are covered with young ash trees, together with plenty of birch and hazel. Early in spring the yellow-green hazel catkins make lovely patches of colour against the bare trees. Where the stream bends away from the path there are little clearings where the trees are hung with honeysuckle whose leaves, like the hazel catkins, appear very early in the season.

About 200 metres from the car park you cross the river by a new wooden bridge. The granite boulders in the stream bed were carried by a local glacier from a few miles up the valley and smoothed and rounded by the water. The slopes of the hill beyond the bridge have ferns in plenty: male fern and hartstongue. The ground is carpeted with cushions of bright yellow-green moss with darker green shoots of wild garlic amongst them, its white, star-like flowers appearing in April and a lovely smell coming from the leaves. Where the stream bends away from the path there are little clearings where the trees are hung with honeysuckle whose leaves, like the hazel catkins, appear very early.

The path begins to rise soon, passing by laurels and later by the pale green-stemmed shrub *Leycesteria*, both of them remnants of the days when the wood was a private demesne. Before long the path forks: the right-hand turn leads to a second bridge which allows a quick return to the car park. The left fork goes by a muddy way up a tributary stream and past a grove of hawthorn.

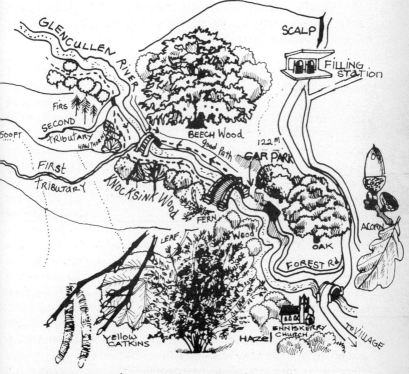

Knocksink Wood

This leads to a knoll high above the main river and the beginnings of a distant view as the valley widens. A perilously slithery descent brings you across a second tributary and out of the old woodland to a new plantation of Douglas fir. From here a very steep climb goes high up the side of the valley and leaves an open way upstream towards Glencullen Bridge.

This path continues through the forest for a mile or so, but our route goes back on its tracks as far as the second bridge. Crossing it takes you to the left bank and a good path passing below an old beech wood with tall trees on a steep slope. Beeches are beautiful, but they come into leaf quickly and cast a dense shade which prevents smaller plants from growing beneath them. The ground on the hillside here is mainly mud, in contrast to the green carpet of the ash thicket. From the beeches a walk of a few minutes brings you back to the car park.

---

42   THE EARL'S DRIVE

This is one of a number of signposted walking routes approached from the third car park on the Long Hill road as you go southwards from Enniskerry. The routes are shown by arrows of various colours, the Earl's being black. An excellent place for dogs and children.

Powerscourt Paddock is a large tract of land on the eastern slopes of Djouce Mountain. The upper part of the valley was filled by two beautiful man-made ponds, devised as part of the landscaping of the estate in the 19th century. At first there was just one lake, planned by Tom Parnell, an uncle of Charles Stewart. However, as the 7th Viscount Powerscourt wrote, 'Mr Parnell being occupied with religious meetings in Dublin, the work was carelessly done'. In 1841 or 1842 the dam collapsed.

His lordship restored the lake, but felt that 'the flood pressure of the water would be less if the lake were divided into two levels'. This work was completed in 1860 and all was well until the lower dam was destroyed by the floods which accompanied Hurricane Charlie in 1986. It has been replaced by a causeway, carrying the forest road over a concrete culvert.

In the car park, the pale, silvery-green trees amongst the darker spruces are noble firs. In summer, their lower branches are festooned with little brown male cones hanging downwards while, on the higher branches, the big, cylindrical female cones stand stiffly upright. A path leads steeply downhill through the trees towards the water, passing first through spruce and then through larches. It takes a sharp bend near the bottom of the hill and straightens out to follow the lake margin.

The southern end of the lake is filled by a curious green, grassy mound surrounded by rushes. Apparently the stream forked at

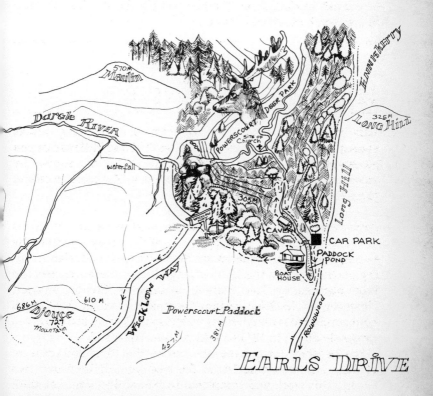

this point. As the years went by, silt accumulated and created an island, standing above a rushy swamp. The surviving pond is shallow and has an abundant growth of a red-leaved pondweed. In summer there are also clumps of the tall, pale green leaves of water plantain standing out above the surface. The water is much richer than in the usual County Wicklow lakes so that plants and animals abound and there is plenty of food for fish.

The rock outcrop beside the first dam is quartzite, the material which forms the ridge of Long Hill. The flanks of the hill are of slate which the rivers have eroded to form a gorge between Long Hill on one side and Djouce on the other. Down at the bottom lies the level ground of Powerscourt deerpark.

Between the path and the bank of the lower pond native trees, mountain ash and holly, have seeded themselves while the upper slopes have been planted with larch. Just below the larch, wild flowers thrive in the shelter: gorse and ling heather, woodsage and frochan. The yellow, dandelion-like flower which blooms in summer is catsear, named from the tiny grey, scale-like leaves on the stem.

Across the valley you can see the sad and lonely boat-house, high above the stream, eternally yawning with the frustration of no longer being able to shelter a boat. The pond curves so that, as you round the bend, you have a sudden and splendid view across the deerpark to the summit of Maulin.

A short diversion at the dam, down the hill on the right bank, brings you to an outcrop of the slate, in this region distinguished by its bright, reddish purple colour. But the route takes you across the valley to turn right and right again where the road forks and the Earl's Drive takes you down the valley. The Earl was Lord Roden, grandfather of the 7th Viscount Powerscourt. Tom Parnell planned the road with a gentle slope so that a horse could trot up or down hill on it. There are side valleys, the first of which gives a view across to Carrigoona, the small rocky hill to the north of the Sugarloaf.

Then comes a deep cleft with a waterfall which drops into a wonderful cavern, its entrance walls festooned with hard fern, male fern, damp mosses and leafy liverworts. The water flows into the cavern which is damp and dark and slithery underfoot.

Bring a torch if you want to explore it, though it doesn't seem to go very far.

The big birch tree across the path from the cavern grows from the top of an old stone bridge built to carry the drive over the ravine. From this point onwards, red cedars line the sides of the way which now zig-zags gently down the side of the valley, passing by foxgloves which stand more than six feet tall. The second zig gives a lovely view over the Dargle where it meanders along the floor of the deerpark and you can hear the roar of the waterfalls.

There is a slightly confusing place where the black arrows seem to point in both directions. The right-pointing one is a short-cut: the left takes you on down to the river where it flows over gravel, pebbles and boulders. All are relatively bare, with little plant growth and are the spoil of Hurricane Charlie. Here you enter a pinewood and in a little while must ford the stream to continue the path up the valley, passing a great boulder of errant granite and an outcrop of the local slate.

So to deep dark woods of spruce on a path which brings you up the hill to pick up the trail where the shortcut led. About half way up the hill, you can see down to a secluded waterfall where crystal clear water cascades into a deep pool. Then you meet the outgoing path close to the old dam.

Between the path and the upper pond stand ancient and decaying beech trees with younger oaks and sycamore. The seclusion of the Paddock Pond, so close to a busy mountain road is delightful. You can sit in a silence broken only by the splash of trout rising amongst the pondweed and the song of willow warblers and chaffinches. At the southern end, normal civilised life begins again abruptly, with sheep pasture and farm cottages: quite picturesque but almost seeming to intrude on a half-forgotten world in the valley.

43 THE GLEN OF THE DOWNS

The Dublin to Wicklow bus passes through the Glen. Entrance to car park marked by Forestry sign 'Bellevue Wood', 9 km south of Kilmacanogue. A safe and delightful walk for children and dogs. The marked route runs for a little under 3 km.

The carpark in the Glen of the Downs makes a very pleasant resting place on the busy road between Bray and Wicklow. The curtain of trees effectively cuts off the view of traffic and numerous footpaths allow you to wander along the banks of the Three Trout Stream on the floor of the valley or climb the steep, wooded slopes above. The Glen itself is a glacial 'overflow channel', excavated by torrential rivers of meltwater when the ice sheets were receding and temporary dams prevented rivers from following their normal routes.

A route beginning north of the car park leads to the highest point on the hillside. The trail on the map is a gentle one and stays mainly on the lower ground. Turning right after entering the car park brings you to a recently made clearing which used to be a grove of laurels. They are the remnants of 19th century landscape gardening and have survived the return to the wilderness which has overtaken most of the Glen.

One of the most puzzling features of the Glen is the scree at Stop 20 of the Nature Trail. Such heaps of rock fragments are common enough on high mountains and at the bases of cliffs. But here the mountain is not high and the hill, although steep, scarcely qualifies as a cliff. The rock fragments are pale coloured, greenish or yellowish lumps of quartzite.

Apart from a few determined pennyworts amongst the stones, the scree is devoid of plant life. An oak tree makes a sort of island within it and in the shelter the ground is peaty and covered with ling heather. Frochans grow above the scree and an extraordinary sward of the fern polypody grows below it. At the sides, honeysuckle and brambles, rooted in the soil, spread over the stones where they are free from any competing plants. After the scree, you pass through a thicket of beech, birch and ash and take

BEECH

HOLLY

ASH

CAR PARK

To BRAY

LAUREL GROVE

PENNYWORT PLANT

SCREE

OAK ACORN.

OAK WOOD

THREE TROUT

SCOTS PINE

STREAM

Eucalyptus

To WICKLOW

The Glen of the Downs

FIR

NORWAY MAPLE TREES

YEW TREE

GOLF STEPS. LINKS

ROCK OUTCROP

SHELTER

STREAM

131

the uphill slope at a picnic table.

As the path goes higher, oaks begin to take over the forest. Up to medieval times, oak wood clothed most of the slopes of the Wicklow Mountains. In the course of the past few centuries, the trees have been felled. In some favoured places, those which grew up again from stumps survived the final phases of deforestation. By that time, beech and other exotic trees had gained a foothold so that the Glen of the Downs is not a perfect example of primeval woodland – but it certainly gives a good impression of the appearance of the ancient state of Ireland, the sort of view that would have greeted natives and settlers up to the 16th century.

After the oaks comes a plantation of Scots pine, fine tall trees with orange-red trunks. Pines did exist in Ireland as native plants but are generally believed to have had a period of extinction, before being replaced with imports from Scotland. The ground beneath them is littered in places with the cores of chewed pine cones, showing the presence of plenty of squirrels up above.

Just beyond the pines, the green turf of Delgany golf links makes a sharp contrast with the woodland. This marks a geological boundary: the forest grows on acid soil derived from the underlying rock while the golf links lie on more fertile gravels deposited by the Irish Sea glacier.

Stop 13 on the Nature Trail marks a lovely, spreading yew: like oak and holly it is one of our rather few native species of tree. Farther on, steps have been provided, partly out of kindness to wayfarers, but also to protect the steep slope beneath from the erosion which would result from indiscriminate scramblings.

The return journey begins at a shelter, made from the remains of a house, surrounded by a long-forgotten garden. Outcrops of the Bray slates which lie beneath the soil appear on the right of the path. Beyond these the road rises and the trees include a rare plantation of Norway maple, its pale bark distinguishing it from the sycamores nearby. After them you meet a group of eucalyptus and then the path descends to the pleasant jungle of self-sown trees.

44 LUGGALA WOOD

Sallygap is approached from Dublin through Rathfarnham and Glencree. The nearest bus is St Kevin's to Roundwood, 5 km away. Ideal for dogs and children, the walk takes an hour at a gentle pace.

The road from Sallygap to Roundwood is very beautiful, passing through some of the finest mountain and cliff scenery in Ireland. Many people are aware of this and the combination of popularity with narrowness makes the same road hazardous for drivers attempting to admire the view. Fortunately, several car parks have been provided by the Forest Service and these give access to uncrowded, shady footpaths leading to the mountainside.

Luggala Wood is entered from the first car park which you meet on the high ground above Lough Tay on the road from Sally Gap. The forest entrance is marked by a post and rail fence and cars are barred from it by a boom attached to two gateposts.

The posts display convenient specimens of the local stone. The dramatic scenery results from the fact that the valley below lies at the edge of the granite mass of the Wicklow Mountains. Chemical action between the older strata to the east and the granite magma to the west transformed the old rock to the bright, flakey mica schist.

Most of the stones in the gateway are schist, greenish or brown with a very fine-grained structure. There are a few blocks of quartz, stained pale brown by the iron in the groundwater. The quartz was deposited in fissures formed not long after the earth movements which created the mountains. Finally, there are two or more specimens of granite, a much more coarsely grained stone than the schist, speckled black and white.

The trees are mainly Sitka spruce which thrives on the damp, peaty soil derived from schist and granite. Well grown now, they cast a welcome shade on a hot day and you can plunge into the silence of the forest, screened after a few minutes' walk from the road and its traffic.

The steep sides of the path are damp and generally unsuitable for higher plants to grow. Their places are taken by a variety of mosses: *Polytrichum* which resembles a miniature fir tree and *Sphagnum* which is low-growing and spongy. Thousands of years ago, when rainfall was greater, mosses such as these grew so luxuriantly that they formed blanket peat and took over the forest.

Half a mile up the hill, the path cutting makes a section through the peat and the stumps of conquered trees are still preserved after some five thousand years. The acid moisture of the peat prevents the bacterial action which would normally digest the tree stumps.

The path ends abruptly in a clearing where tall spruces surround you on all sides. A stream rushes down through it, over miniature waterfalls in a cool, dark place. The rocks are stained pale brown by iron and the submerged ones are covered with a thin coating of algae. The forest is too dark and the water too soft to allow larger water plants to grow.

If you turn over stones in the stream you may find some of the creatures which live in this rather inhospitable region. Green, caterpillar-like creatures which live on the undersides of loose stones try to wriggle away out of the light. They are the larvae of caddis flies and live beneath the surface of the stream for a year before hatching into delicate, moth-like insects.

The clearing is carpeted with grasses and rushes, but the tree canopy above is too dense to allow them to grow within the wood. Instead, anywhere a gleam of light can get through the trees, there are ferns which enjoy the shelter and the lack of competition from more vigorous, but light-demanding plants.

The clearing makes a pleasant place to end an ascent of a mile or so, but you can continue up a pathway through the trees to the edge of the forest and on up the slopes of Djouce. The return journey down the same path gradually brings you back to the outside world: first the rocky summit of Knocknacloghoge and gradually more and more of the hills and valleys of the Wicklow Mountains.

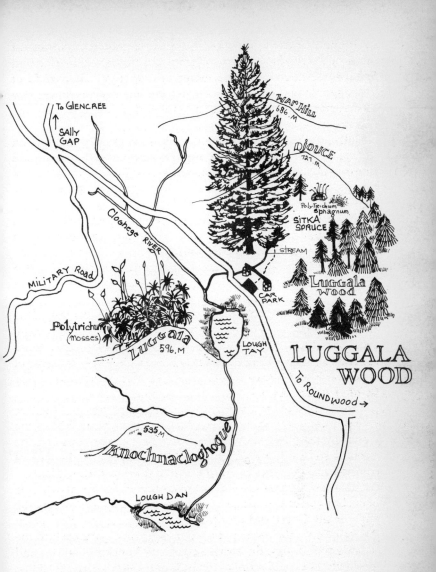

To GLENCREE

SALLY GAP

Cloghege River

MILITARY Road

Polytrichum (mosses)

LUGGALA 596.M

War Hill 686.M

DJOUCE 727.M

Poly-Trichum Sphagnum

SITKA SPRUCE

STREAM

CAR PARK

LOUGH TAY

Luggala Wood

LUGGALA WOOD

To ROUNDWOOD →

535.M

Knochnacloghogue

LOUGH DAN

135

45   THE DEVIL'S GLEN

Turn off the Dublin to Wicklow road in Ashford at the signpost to Glendalough and then follow 'Devil's Glen' signs heading to the road which runs (or climbs) to the south of the Glen. The entrance is a little over 3 km from Ashford. The walk is good for dogs and well-disciplined children. Children of the other kind will find wonderful cliffs to fall down.

His Satanic Majesty may be credited with excellent taste in his selection of scenery for an abode, his Glen being one of the greater glories of County Wicklow. What is more, it lies so far from the main mountain roads that it remains the exclusive territory of the more determined class of picnickers. The Glen is a deep gorge of the Vartry River which was diverted eastwards from its original course by glacial action.

More than a mile of Forestry road brings you from the forest entrance to the car park, travelling just at the edge of the wood. From the car park you can see the facade of Glanmore Castle, designed by Francis Johnston and built about 1804 for Francis Synge, great-grandfather of John Millington, whose uncle inherited the estate. The castle is now an hotel and restaurant. Its setting is wonderful, perched high on the side of the gorge.

The Forest Service have laid out a nature trail which is signposted from the car park. Our route begins by following the nature trail but leaves it for a longer journey to the waterfall at the head of the Glen. The far side of the valley at the beginnings of the trail is a magnificent grey cliff plunging down to the river below. You can hear the river, but it runs hidden amongst the trees. The rock is ancient, belonging to the special Devil's Glen Formation of the Cambrian Bray Series: well over 500 million years old.

The trees by the path are mainly oaks, old and young. Oak is the dominant native tree of the Glen. The ancestors of the present ones have been felled for timber over many generations. But they are once again asserting themselves and the steep slopes bear quite a close resemblance to primeval Irish woodlands.

However, there are some exotics including fine old beeches which may date from the time of the building of the castle. Afforestation in more recent times has introduced the Douglas fir with smooth, grey bark and lovely dark green, shining needles.

Signpost 3 of the nature trail stands opposite to the Himalayan shrub *Leycesteria formosa* with green stem and leaves which contrast in winter with the leafless native bushes. With rhododendrons and laurels it once ornamented the path which was built on the steep hillside in the great days of the demesne. The ground between the trees is densely covered with woodrush, a grass-like plant with broad, shiny leaves. Its presence is sure evidence of the former existence of native oak forest.

Signpost 11 on the trail is below one of the rock outcrops which is covered with a wonderful blanket of lower plants. There are masses of pale grey-green branching lichens and soft cushions of yellow-green moss. They look their best in winter, giving a lovely splash of delicate colours, becoming less noticeable in summer when everything else is green. You leave the nature trail

at a signpost for the Waterfall and follow the path which turns westwards a little farther on, passing Scots pines standing sentinel at the corner.

The Vartry flows from west to east in a straight line here for one kilometre. The path follows the gorge, about 70 metres above the river. The far side of the valley is densely wooded. The trees are mainly oaks with dark brown trunks, but amongst them in winter ashes stand out, nearly white in contrast with finger-like branches.

The path takes you through a short tunnel cut in a rock which stood in the way of the ladies and gentlemen of times long gone. A little way past it, there is an extraordinary growth of ivy which hangs down and has developed exceptionally thick free branches. Farther on you meet a signpost which points towards the waterfall and, shortly afterwards, the road heads downhill. A side stream hurtling down the rock talks to you in a shrill voice, in contrast to the deep rumble of the main river below. At the bottom of the hill you meet the Vartry itself and a lower pathway.

The Vartry here is a lovely river, flowing over great boulders of grey or purple slates which make innumerable pools and eddies. Young ash trees grow by its banks and a dipper lives nearby. The path ends abruptly at the waterfall, giving an unusual sense of having come to the end of the world. Even though the fall is not particularly deep, its top seems to meet the sky.

So you turn back. There are other routes through the woods but they can be confusing and it is safer to take the easier alternative of following the same path in reverse, or possibly to branch off for a lower path which follows the river more closely. Any time of the year is good for the Devil's Glen but perhaps it is best in spring when the wild cherries are in bloom.

Avondale lies a little way off the Dublin to Wexford road, signposted from the crossroads just south of Rathdrum. The walks are safe for children, dogs should be kept under control.

The forest garden of Avondale is one of the most delightful places in Ireland for a peaceful walk. Tall trees cover the slopes of the valley of the Avonmore, providing a screen to shut out all the noisier elements of 20th century civilisation.

Avondale has a remarkable tradition of endeavour in forestry. Samuel Hayes, who built the house in 1777, published a 'Practical Treatise' on forestry in 1794. He introduced many exotic trees and also planted the native species. Charles Stewart Parnell continued the good work, rightly believing in the need to encourage the production of Irish timber. After his death these endeavours suffered a hideous eclipse when the butcher who bought the estate disposed of practically all the trees.

Fortunately, he sold up before long. The demesne was acquired by the Government and the experimental forest garden was planned and executed with remarkable speed. Some of the trees were given generous space to allow them to show their graces as individuals; others were confined to make dense forests so that timber production could be assessed. Between them lie open green swards and footpaths so numerous that you can find one to follow in solitude even on a fine Sunday.

A number of routes have been signposted through the estate and nature trail leaflets are available. One of the longer ones, the Exotic Tree Trail, begins a little way to the south of Avondale House. The home of Parnell during his great days, it has been well restored by the Office of Public Works and is open to visitors.

The path towards the trail from the car park passes the stump of a wind-blown beech tree, labelled with notable dates since its planting in 1734. Rooks used to nest in the branches until 1969, when they departed, having sensed that it was no longer fit for avian habitation. It fell in 1972. The tree was already old when

Avondale

AVONMORE RIVER

Scots Pine

Yew.

Mon[key]
Puz[zle]

LOVERS LEAP

PARNELLS HOUSE

Hollies

BEECHES

Eucalypts 1911

Duck Pond

1734–1972
Old Beech Stump

AUGUST[us]
HENR[Y]
memo[rial]
Flower[s]

CAR PARK

LEAF OF EUCAL[YPTUS]

140

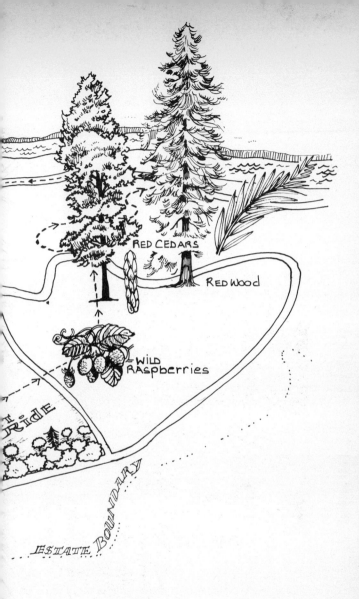

RED CEDARS

REDWOOD

WILD RASPberries

Ride

ESTATE BOUNDARY

Parnell was born in sight of it in 1846.

The slopes of the valley were first planted with forest trees by Samuel Hayes in the 18th century. Few of these survived decimation after the death of Parnell, and the modern planting began in 1907. At that time the estate was planned to allow the study of the growth performance of trees under Irish conditions, both for ornament and as timber producers.

Over the last few years, a great many of the specimens have been labelled, and the first steps of the nature trails are seen to lead past a remarkable variety of hollies. After them come some not so old beeches which have seeded themselves, and then a group of tall eucalypts, planted in 1911. A faint aroma of the eucalyptus oil rises from the ground as you crunch over pink, brown and yellow fallen leaves.

At the edge of this wood, beyond a clump of rhododendrons, a memorial stone inscribed to Augustine Henry stands. He was one of the founding fathers of modern Irish forestry, and the grove of shrubs and trees behind the memorial are varieties either discovered by him or in which he had a particular interest. The trail then plunges briefly into a dark forest of hemlock spruce which has invaded a plot of elms.

The path emerges from the darkness to one of the most imposing parts of Avondale. Called the Great Ride, it is a lovely sward of mown grass, plunging down the valley and climbing up the far slope. On either side is a straight wall of forest, with a row of solitary trees planted a little way out from the others. Each of the solitary specimens stands in front of a one-acre plot of its own species. Or, at any rate, it used to. In the course of time some of the plots failed and were invaded by the more viable species such as spruces and beech.

Eighty years after planting, the majority of the trees have survived. They are lovely to look at and have provided a wealth of information to the science of forestry. The finest of all are the conifers, particularly a Sitka spruce on the left and a silver fir on the right, its fronds like crinolines.

Turning off to the left, just before meeting these giants, leads past wild raspberries towards a deep green dell. After this comes a wood of red cedars and then the roar of the river can be heard in the distance.

A winding path goes gently down a steep slope through giant redwoods to an ancient silver fir which marks the most southerly point of our expedition. This great tree is probably a survivor of the planting by Samuel Hayes in the 18th century.

From the silver fir a roadway runs parallel to the river, where it tumbles over rocky boulders between steep banks. A signpost inscribed 'River Walk' leads to less steep banks where you can sit and watch trout leaping and expect to see a dipper, the beautiful black bird with white breast which lives by sparkling streams. Back on the main path, dark woods give way suddenly to an open slope below the great house, planted with pines and cedars well spaced out on the lawn. The path rises steeply, following the edge of the valley, to bring you level with the tips of tall fir trees and then under a sloping yew to Lover's Leap.

This is a promontory of diorite rock, one of many intrusions of magma which forced their way in through weak points in the surrounding slate. From the Leap you can gaze straight down on the Avonmore, winding its way among the trees a hundred feet below.

That is nearly the end of the journey. The forest walk returns to tarmac and cars, though you might divert to look at the deer in the enclosures on the right beyond the duck pond. It is hard to believe that the forest is almost as much a work of man as is the car-park and its inhabitants.